Living For Another World

A Fresh Blueprint for Today's Authentic Christian

Justin Kendrick

Living For Another World

A Fresh Blueprint for Today's Authentic Christian

Cover Design by Jon Wisecarver and Holyfire Ministries
Edited by Brittany Everett /Layout by Kate DeCiccio

Holyfire Ministries
P.O. Box 3182
New Haven CT 06515
www.holyfireministries.com
www.outofhidingmusic.com
www.agenerationtransformed.blogspot.com

ISBN 978-1-935298-27-4   10 digit 1-935298-27-5

First printing 2009

Printed in the United States of America

Truth Book Publishers
824 Bills Rd
Franklin, IL 62638
877-649-9092
www.truthbookpublishers.com

To my wife, Christina Rose. This book exists because of your ongoing sacrifice.

To my sons. My greatest desire is to model for you the Jesus I write about.

And to my team. It is an honor to take the journey with you.

CONTENTS

INTRODUCTION 9

PART 1 : NEW EYES
Seeing Life Differently 15
CHAPTER 1
The Emergency 17
CHAPTER 2
Changing Priorities 35
CHAPTER 3
Finding the Real You 69
CHAPTER 4
Becoming Intentional 91

PART 2: A NEW ROAD
Practices of an Awakened Life 111
CHAPTER 5
The Garden 113
CHAPTER 6
How to Get the World's Attention 143
CHAPTER 7
Trying Something Impossible.........................171
CHAPTER 8
Pursuing the Fullness 197

NOTES 211

INTRODUCTION

I recently attended a huge concert with thousands of people and five popular bands. The MC for the night was a famous rocker with all the passion and the style you would expect. He wasn't touring with his band anymore and he wasn't coming out with any new albums. He had the look, and the connections, but something was stopping him from hitting the road again with his group. After singing and touring for years, this singer had permanently damaged his voice. I listened to him struggle through the introduction of each group while his scratchy, broken voice echoed throughout the arena. I felt kind of bad for him—that he couldn't pursue his passion in music. He was a singer without a voice to sing.

As I sat in the arena surrounded by thousands of people, my thoughts brought me somewhere else, and I saw the church. I don't mean one church, or a particular denomination. I mean those who seek to represent Jesus to the world around them from every culture group and every sector of society. I specifically thought of the western church. We've got some big buildings, a few TV programs, and all the talent in the world, but somewhere along the line, we lost the ability to radically impact the culture around us. We've lost our voice.

It's true that the church has kept on talking, but little by little the world around us is not stopping to listen. The influence of Christianity on our culture is slipping dramatically and if there is not an immediate change in direction we will fall further and further into irrelevance. Where did the disease start? I don't know. But I think we have reached a season of change and God wants to show us how to change things.

I've found the same ache in the eyes of Christian leaders from every stream and denomination that I find in my own heart. It's a desire for something more than what we've seen in our Sunday morning routines. It's a desire to see things change in a big way, to make things real, and to get back to the core of our faith. You're probably reading this book because you have that same aching desire. We can't just continue to float along with business as usual. Something needs to fundamentally shift or turn...

But what?

I think that the answer is found in the supreme court of scripture: the words of Jesus. Two thousand years ago, He stood in a room with one of the most powerful Roman officials of His age and whispered the secret that we have lost in our generation, just as they had lost it in theirs. Alone with Pontius Pilate, the Son of God explained the overarching theme of His entire life. He said, "My kingdom is not of this world" (John 18:36).

Why are those words so important and what do they have to do with our problems today? This one sentence from the Son of God exposes two things: His perspective and His priorities. And it's these two things that we have lost. Most of us are keenly aware of the fact that the American church needs spiritual CPR, but our solution to awakening the church has been to introduce new structures to revive it. We have denominational churches and non-denominational churches, house churches, and small groups, emerging churches, and seeker sensitive churches, pyramid schemes, or leadership classes, membership cards, and a thousand other structural changes that are important and sometimes necessary –but never deal with the core problem that we are facing.

I believe that the core deficiency is one of substance. Although structure is important and strategic, substance is the missing piece of our faith and our communities. Somewhere along the line, we lost the substance of the kingdom.

This book will focus on the premise that the reality of the kingdom and the practice of living for another world are the key components that need to be restored in the lives of Christians of our generation. If they are not restored, I don't believe that followers of Jesus will have a voice in our world. But if they are restored, then this world will hear and experience the truth that Jesus lived, died and rose again to express. And they will hear it through you and me.

I want to warn you that some of the things I share in this book haunt me at times. Many of the truths I express are real, and urgent, and often forgotten, and all have the ability to change the way everything else in life looks. I'm not a college professor and I've never pastored a church. I have a tremendous amount of respect for leaders in the body of Christ from all different streams and I wrote this book because I couldn't get away from the burning desire to share with you the reality that was progressively setting me free. Other incredible books have been written on the subjects that I will discuss and my writing is not an attempt to replace them. As we stand together as followers of Jesus, my desire is only to add these thoughts to the conversation.

I have written this book primarily to the Christian who has grown tired of ordinary life and grown desperately hungry for the miracle-working, mountain-shaking power that Jesus promised. This is for the follower of Jesus who is still willing to dream and who is still willing to take risks. If you find yourself unsatisfied with normal life, then it is my prayer that God will use these pages to provoke you to an entirely new way of living.

Part 1

New Eyes

SEEING LIFE DIFFERENTLY

Maybe you've heard the story of the elephant and the chain. From the time the elephant was very young, its owner put a chain around its neck and fastened that chain to a pole cemented deep in the ground. For days, the young elephant pulled against the chain but it could not break free. Then the day came when the elephant decided to stop pulling. From that day forward, whenever the owner tied the chain around his neck, the elephant would not pull against it.

Today the elephant is full-grown. If he wanted to, he could pull almost any stake from the ground. However, because of his training, the owner can fasten the chain to a small wooden stake, gently tap that stake into the dirt, and the elephant will not pull against it. The elephant doesn't need more power or more strength to be free from the chain. He just needs a clear view of reality.

The first part of this book is dedicated to seeing things differently. For too long, you and I have been the elephant. We've got all the power and potential in the world, but our chains still keep us bound. If we can re-prioritize our lives based upon God's perspective rather than our own, we will start to see the powerful results that God promises. I want to warn you: Seeing things differently can really mess up your current way of living.

Chapter 1
THE EMERGENCY

I remember the day like it was yesterday. It was a day that forever changed the way I look at life. The date was June 18th, 2007. It was sunny and warm—perfect weather for a drive. I was heading home from 11 days of ministry throughout the Adirondack region of upstate New York with eight of my closest friends. My wife and son were with me. The night before, our ministry team had taken communion together and thanked God for the hundreds of people who had been touched by His power throughout the trip. That morning, the nine of us jumped in to our 36-foot long motor home and began the six-hour journey back to Connecticut. We had no idea how much that day had in store.

Only forty-five minutes into the trip, while traveling down Route 73 East in the middle of the mountains, our motor home started stinking of exhaust. We had been having problems with the engine and talked with a number of mechanics about the problems. It was just serviced a few weeks earlier and we had arranged with the shop to drop it off again as soon as we got home. On the top of a mountain, overlooking the quaint little town of Keene Valley, our group decided to pull over to the side of the road and get some fresh air.

Once the nine of us had gotten out of the motor home and stretched our legs, we noticed a slight hiss coming from the engine. It grew louder and louder until it sounded like fireworks were going off under the hood. Within minutes, flames shot out of the front grill and the fire lapped around the sides of the bus. Afraid of an explosion, we all began to move away from the engine. It didn't take long before the flames soared 35 feet into the air and the motor home was completely engulfed in the fire. We scrambled for our cell phones to call for help. Most of us had left them on the vehicle, and those who had them didn't have any reception. As we stood overlooking the mountains, alone in the middle of nowhere, the emergency set in. Our instruments, luggage, computers, cell phones, and dozens of other personal items went up in a blaze of ash and smoke and we were paralyzed—unable to do anything. It didn't take long. We lost over fifty thousand dollars in possessions in just under forty minutes.

Eventually someone saw the fire and drove to the nearest town to report it. I remember when the Keene Valley Fire Department finally arrived. It was one guy, dressed in civilian clothes in a pick-up truck. By the time fire engines got there, the motor home had nearly burnt down to the tires. Once they put the fire out, one of the firefighters pulled me aside and told me that it was our lucky day. If we had reached the crest of the mountain and started the downward descent, we would have been heading downhill for miles with nowhere to pull over. It was likely that we would have lost our breaks on the way down.

I've often wondered how things would be different if we hadn't stopped to get some fresh air on June 18th. I think about holding the hand of my one-year-old son as we lose our breaks going down the mountain. I don't think about it long.

Have you ever experienced an emergency? I'm sure you have. There's something about it that changes your perspective. It definitely has the power to make you look at things differently. Most of the time, we live our lives in "normal mode," shuffling through the various aspects of our routine. Every once in a while, something shakes our reality and we are pushed in to "emergency mode." I'm sure you've experienced the feeling. Maybe a family member passed away, or you witnessed a terrible accident or crime. Maybe a house burned down on your street or your friend's dad died unexpectedly.

Emergency mode is kind of like changing the color settings on your TV. Everything is tainted by the experience. Your heart beats faster. You're more aware. The things that were important in normal mode now they look petty and insignificant. Life takes on a different meaning.

These are the moments when timid people become courageous and when selfish people give their lives for someone else. It's almost like we are shaken from our sleep, and the emergency has this power to convert us into something grander and more noble. The problem is that life has a tendency to flip back into normal mode once the emergency has calmed down. We forget about our neighbors and get back to living for what we want out of life never allowing the experience to permanently change the way we live.

But what if there was an emergency that was so big, and so urgent, and so important that it demanded your attention every day for the rest of your life? And what if the emergency was worth that kind of sacrifice? If it was real, and if it was true, and if it profoundly affected those whom you love most, would you be willing to make the kind of change the emergency required?

This chapter is dedicated to seeing the war that rages around us. I am convinced that it's the most serious epidemic in the history of humanity. It is not a physical, financial, or economical epidemic. It has nothing to do with political changes or market changes. It is far bigger than these things. The epidemic is not a religious one. We have millions of churches sprinkled through every town and every state of our nation. The problem is not that we've lost our spirituality or our religion. The problem is that in the midst of our efforts, we have lost the most important thing. Simply put, people no longer see Jesus in Christians. We have stopped living for another world.

The epidemic has created a society that has the wrong impression of God. Christians share about the love of Jesus, but unbelievers feel like they already know the routine. They've heard it a million times. They've read the tract, went to the service, watched the movie, and went home unchanged. What they want to find, but too often never do, is a transformed life—a person that embodies the message.

They want to see someone who works from a completely different playbook and plays by completely different rules. They want to find someone who really lives like they believe in Heaven, Hell, sin and judgment. Instead, most unbelievers find people very much like themselves, who live for their sports teams, paychecks and their media addictions. Jesus is just another compartment in their life.

A distorted concept of Jesus is a thousand times more lethal than no concept of Him at all, and today we face a young generation that has seen decades of this distorted view of what it means to follow Jesus. They've watched as parents and grandparents have lived double lives and the world's greatest preachers have come crashing down. They've watched as their families have fallen apart—and they've been left to pick up the pieces.

This bitterness has led to a culture where people want to define their own version of right and wrong. We've grown weary of others forcing their rules upon us, so an entire generation has learned to treat truth like a grocery store, picking and choosing the rules they want to embrace. The problem with this attitude is that it only spreads the disease.

THE FOUNDATION IS GONE

My four years in college were a crash course in realizing the emergency. I attended Southern Connecticut State University with about 12,000 other students, nestled in the heart of New England. The Christian fellowship that I was a part of on campus was the only Christian club at the school and we had about 50 members. Needless to say, it was not the most Jesus-friendly, Bible-loving atmosphere. I can still remember living in the dorms and joking with my friends that if we stayed in the hallway too long we would get high off the marijuana smoke seeping out from under our neighbor's doors.

In my senior year, I took a social work course that focused on diversity and social trends. It wasn't long before we landed on the topic of homosexuality. The professor wanted to hear our views on this hotly debated social issue. That particular day in class, I was seated between two girls who were very open about their lives as homosexuals. As different students shared their views on the topic, I could feel a lump the size of a tennis ball begin to develop in my throat. With all my heart, I love every person God created on this planet and I have no hate or prejudice towards homosexuals. That being said, I believe that homosexuality is a sin. I believe that it's one of many crafty lies that have deceived our culture.

How was I going to share my honest, loving, viewpoint in a way that didn't inspire the rest of the class to tie me up and hang me from the ceiling? Other students knew that I was a Christian, and I felt like they were all starting to perk up, waiting to see how I would respond. The awkwardness was palpable. Finally, shaking inside, I raised my hand. The professor called on me and I began to state my case. "I don't agree with the homosexual lifestyle," I said.

The temperature of the room went up fifty degrees as soon as I spoke those words. Students started shifting in their seats and the professor became noticeably uneasy. I think someone coughed just to break the awkward moment. "What do you mean by that?" probed the professor.

I continued, "Well, I am a Christian and I believe that the Bible is completely true. I believe it's inspired by God and it explains how human beings should live, so I've chosen to align my beliefs with its truth claims. The Bible teaches that homosexuality is not the way God designed us to live or act and He calls it sin." I thought at this point someone was going to flip over a desk and start screaming that I was a religious bigot. The reaction I received, however, was unexpected. It wasn't anger or rage that I saw in the faces of the other students or the professor. Instead, the response was one of complete and absolute bewilderment. You know the look that your dog gives you when you make a high-pitched whistling sound and their ears perk up—it was a little like that.

They all sat there looking at me as if I had just given my response in an African dialect that uses clicking and popping noises. They couldn't fathom the idea that an honors student at the university would actually draw his values from an ancient book written thousands of years ago. This concept was completely foreign to anything they had ever seriously considered.

I knew that most people in my class had never read the Bible and didn't really care what it said, but I didn't know that they had never considered living life based on a set of absolute truths—even when those truths are not particularly convenient to believe. They saw faith as something you add to life to help, not a worldview to base your life upon. This classroom was a microcosm of our world. People say that they believe in God, but that's very different than actually believing and following the Bible. Believing in God is not the same as accepting the values laid out in scripture as our own foundation for what's right and wrong. Instead of a Biblical foundation, this generation has replaced it with the grocery store method. Most young people don't actually believe anything—not absolutely, at least. Ron Luce, in his book, *Battle Cry for a Generation,* mentions a recent study that shows the dramatic change in our views over the last seventy-five years.

-Of those born in the U.S. between 1927-1945, 65% consider themselves Bible-based Christians.
-Of those born in the U.S. between 1946-1964, 35% consider themselves Bible-based Christians.
-Of those born in the U.S. between 1965-1983, 16% consider themselves Bible-based Christians.
-Of those born in the U.S. between 1984-current, 4% consider themselves Bible-based Christians.

People across America are still calling themselves Christians by the millions, but there has been a fundamental change in the way they view the world. This is the fertile ground for the disease to spread, allowing people to maintain the title as a follower of Christ without embracing the values which the title requires. Millions of Christians have decided to abandon the idea that the Bible is the foundation for what is right and wrong because in the eyes of many people, this idea seems archaic and outdated. The reality is that whether we realize it or not, our nation has undergone one of the largest spiritual changes in the history of any culture.

Only 4 percent of this young, upcoming generation even considers themselves Bible-believing Christians. What about the other 96 percent? They are lost somewhere in the murky waters of unbelief or half-belief. The problem goes deeper than a few scary statistics. For thousands of us, sin has been renamed and is now the accepted norm.

Recently, I was sitting in a large waiting room with about fifteen other people. I sat down next to a young girl and her boyfriend. After a few minutes, we started to talk. She asked me what I did for a living and I fumbled through an honest explanation of Jesus, my love for Him, and the fact that I go around sharing that. Then I asked her what she did. The girl looked at me with a twinkle in her eye. She said, "Well, actually, I'm a stripper."

Something inside my heart broke when I heard her say that. I looked at her and said exactly what she didn't expect me to say. "You know, God has something so much better for you. He doesn't want you to take your clothes off for money."

Those words startled her and caused her to launch in to a speech (one that she had probably given before) about all the reasons why she took the job. It paid good, and it didn't really bother her, and she got a lot of attention. As I shared about who Jesus was in my life, something started to change in her expression. Her proud persona cracked and then crumbled, and soon I could see the girl who had been taken advantage of all her life.

The conversation changed as I told her about my relationship with my wife. "We dated for over five years before we were married," I told her, "And we saved sex for marriage." Her mouth hit the floor. She didn't believe me. She had never heard of anyone doing that before. The girl fired question after question to try to get me to tell her it wasn't really true. She thought I was weird and strange for even wanting to wait. After another ten minutes of discussion, she got very quiet and turned away. Then she said something much softer, almost under her breath. She said, "You know, I wish I'd waited."

What's going on here? Why would this girl change her thinking and confess that she should have waited on sex for marriage? The answer is not as complicated as we sometimes think. Sin is sin even when we call it something different and it leads to death every time. It might be death on the inside expressed through emptiness or depression, or it might be death on the outside expressed through destroyed relationships or painful experiences. Either way, we can't fool ourselves for long. Sin still leads to death, and it's deceiving and destroying this generation. The need for change is urgent and desperate—lives are being claimed every day.

We don't have to look far to see the devastation that sin is causing in our generation. If you're like me, you don't need to go beyond your close friends and immediate family to witness the chaos caused by sin. There's the cousin in her early twenties who has had two abortions and lost the parental rights to her baby son. She's addicted to cocaine and is pregnant again. There's the friend from work who is married with four kids and just found out that his wife has been cheating on him. There's the mom or dad who is addicted to pain killers and alcohol. I'm sure that you've thought of three or four people you know who have a story that goes something like one of these.

In his Book, *Revolution*, Dr. Michael Brown reports that since 1960 the American divorce rate has doubled, teen suicide has tripled, reported violent crime has quadrupled, and America's prison population has quintupled. The sins of the fathers fall on the children and those children are now having children. For most of us, it's not something we've just read about. It's not just on TV or in a movie. It's next door, and down the street, and in your own heart.

THE REAL PROBLEM

What is the disease I'm describing? The only way to understand it is to begin and end in the scripture. We are beings created in the image of God. He designed us to be like Him and to operate with His attributes. The core of our humanity understands this, and we inherently know what is right and wrong. The problem is that at the birth of our race, our ancestors chose to disobey God. It didn't just change their lives—it changed their nature, and passed on to every human being a frame that is bent. I learned about bent frames as a teenager when I crashed my Jeep Wrangler. My mechanic told me that if the frame wasn't bent, he could fix the Jeep, but if the frame was bent then I didn't need to repair the vehicle. I needed to replace it.

The greatest need for the human race is not a clear set of rules. It's a new frame. We must experience redemption and become new creatures with new desires and new passions. Education can't do that. Government can't do that. The only cure is the life-transforming power found in the gospel of the kingdom—this is what Jesus came and died to give us and this is, fundamentally, what's been lost. People wear a Christian name tag, but have not been inwardly transformed.

The emergency spreads from here because without followers of Christ offering redemption to a broken world, the world tries to come up with their own form of redemption. From scientific explanations for sin, to prescription drugs intended to fix our imbalances, the problems do not go away. Only Jesus brings redemption and only people who have been truly redeemed can spread His redemptive life.

I look out over the landscape of this generation, and I get the same feeling that I got when I was talking to the girl who worked as a stripper. My heart burns inside me as I see people I love blindly follow the lie. Instead of God being worshipped, celebrities are worshipped. Instead of families being a place of safety, they're often the center of hate and rage. Instead of Christianity being the source of life and hope, it has become for many a museum display, or a pie-in-the-sky fairy tale, or a suppressive, judgmental system.

I want to scream and tell them that they don't need to take off their clothes to make a few bucks. I want to tell them that the hollowness and emptiness they feel is not all there is to life, and that it doesn't have to be such a rollercoaster. I get the feeling that if I don't show them that there's a better way, then who will? If I don't respond to this emergency, then who will respond?

IT CAN'T BE IGNORED

The story of the Titanic has always intrigued me. On March 31st, 1909 construction began on this massive sea vessel and it was soon being called "mankind's greatest achievement on the open sea." It was given the nickname "unsinkable." At 882 feet long and approximately 46,000 tons, the ship outsized and outclassed anything ever created by the human mind. On its maiden voyage, from the coast of Europe to New York City, the ship hit an iceberg and sank. Of the nearly 2,200 people on board, 1,522 died. It was an emergency of historic proportions, and it's sinking sent shockwaves around the world.

The part of the story that most intrigues me is the role of a ship called the California, which was not far from the emergency. When the Titanic radioed the California for help, it received no response. The California had shut it's radio off for the night. As the terror and panic gripped the crew and passengers of the

Titanic, they began shooting flares into the air, hoping to rouse the attention of the nearby ship. The lookout men on the California saw the flares, but noticed how low in the air they were, and assumed that the Titanic must be celebrating rather than calling for help. After all, they thought, the ship was unsinkable.

The California never responded to the Titanic's desperate calls for help and in two and a half hours, the world's greatest ship was completely under the icy sea. The passengers and crew of the California slept peacefully that night while just a few miles away hundreds of people wept, screamed, and died.

I can only imagine the feeling of regret that the crew of the California experienced when they realized that they had ignored the Titanic's desperate plea. I can only imagine the overwhelming sense of responsibility they felt when they realized that they could have done something. It wasn't that they didn't want to help. It was just that they didn't really believe that there was an emergency.

This thought raises a set of questions that have haunted me at times. It challenges the core of who I am and what I live for. Do I really believe that all this "Jesus stuff" is true? Do I really believe in an eternal hell, sin leading to death, and a world that is blind? Do I really believe that I am on this planet to distribute the cure for sin found only in redemption?

How can I say that I believe these things and act with indifference towards the unsaved or the poor? As far as I can tell, these beliefs demand a radical priority shift in my daily actions. If I don't respond to the emergency, then I am officially part of the disease. I'm one of those people who wears the Christian nametag but deceives the world through my un-redeemed life. It's going to take big change. It's going to color the way everything in life looks, and it's definitely going to mess up my current routine. If it doesn't, then I still haven't gotten it.

In the book, *Revolution*, the Barna Research Group found that the typical church-going Christian will die without ever leading a single person to the lifesaving knowledge of Jesus Christ. It's not because there aren't enough Christian books at Barnes and Noble, or there aren't enough preachers on TV. It's because most Christians don't live differently enough to be recognized—and even worse, most Christians don't see anything wrong with the way they live.

The story of the Titanic isn't just a story of tragedy. It's also a story of great heroic faith. Among the 2,200 people on-board the ship, there was a middle-aged man named John Harper. He was a preacher from Great Britain whose wife had just recently died. He boarded the ship with his nine-year old daughter and his eleven-year old niece with hopes of starting a new life in Chicago. When the Titanic hit an iceberg and began to sink, Harper was given a seat in a lifeboat next to his two girls. As the workers lowered down the lifeboat, he realized that this was his moment to respond to the emergency. So he did something unfathomable. He kissed his daughter and his niece, told them that he loved them, and stepped back onto the sinking ship.

Giving up his seat so that someone else could get in the lifeboat, John Harper climbed back on to the deck of the Titanic. He found himself surrounded by the screams and tears of hundreds of passengers. He gave his lifejacket away to someone who didn't have one, and began comforting those who were panicking. Soon a group formed around him and John Harper shared with them the hope of Jesus Christ that had changed him on the inside. Passengers started asking for prayer and within minutes, Harper was leading a group of desperate souls to cry out to Jesus for grace and mercy.

In his moment of testing, there was something inside of John Harper that enabled him to be completely selfless. The emergency had drawn it out of him. From his perspective, the souls of others became more important than his own life. He died that night in those freezing waters, and most people have never heard of John Harper. But maybe he had discovered something that we desperately lack. Maybe he had caught a glimpse of something real.

Chapter 2
CHANGING PRIORITES

Everybody knows of Christopher Columbus. As a kid, you learn the song about how he sailed the ocean blue and discovered America. Although historians debate who should be credited with America's discovery, history has singled out Columbus as the man who gets the credit. On August 3rd, 1492, he left Europe and embarked on his first journey into the uncharted western waters. What he found on that journey, and what would result from his findings, has etched Columbus' name in the walls of history forever.

It wasn't only what Columbus found that made him famous. In fact, many others had found it before him. It was that Christopher Columbus had just the right amount of influence, passion and trustworthiness to convince the world that they had believed a lie. Expecting to run into the shores of Asia, Columbus and his crew soon realized that their journey would be longer than they thought. Many of his men still believed that the earth was flat and as the days at sea passed and there were no signs of Asia in sight, they feared that they would soon reach the end of the earth and fall off. But instead they soon found the shores of a land that had barely been touched by European explorers. Columbus returned to Europe and convinced the people of his continent that there was a new world on the other side of the western sea—and that truth changed history.

This story is a great illustration of what is commonly called a paradigm shift. In fact, Columbus' journey would ultimately spark an historic paradigm shift and change every map in Europe. A paradigm is a set of basic assumptions or a way to view the world. In the case of Columbus, people had two basic assumptions that he would disprove. First, some believed the world was flat. Second, others believed that sailing west from Europe would lead directly to Asia. Those were their paradigms—their ways of explaining the world. When Columbus returned to Spain with news of a new world, he introduced a better way of explaining the earth. It was a new paradigm.

The term "paradigm" began as a word used exclusively for science. Scientists say that a paradigm is the set of assumptions they use to understand or explain the things around us. A paradigm shift takes place when there are a number of occurrences that do not fit into the accepted view of reality. These occurrences are called "anomalies". Columbus' report of a new world was an anomaly and most people were skeptical. As more voyages were taken and more proof was given, people began to let go of their old beliefs and started to accept this new way of seeing the earth's geography.

Social paradigm shifts occur all the time, but most of us usually don't recognize them or call them by that name. Fifteen or twenty years ago, for example, owning a cell phone was almost completely unheard of. The only kid in America who owned a cell phone was Zack Morris, from the TV show *Saved by the Bell*, and his phone was awkwardly huge. Zack kept it in his locker and would pull it out and make a call from time to time. I remember as a young kid asking my brother why Zack kept a phone in his locker. Neither of us knew—we just thought it was weird.

Today, if you walk in to any public high school and ask students to hold up their cell phones, almost every student will reach into their pocket and proudly raise their phone. The standard has changed. Now cell phones are a necessity for most people. Zack Morris had a phone and it was an anomaly, but a paradigm shift occurred in the minds of American youth and now it's common.

Scientists say that with every paradigm shift and once enough anomalies occur, there comes a time to abandon the old paradigm. This leads to a state of crisis, where new paradigms are introduced and finally a better paradigm is accepted. We can see this trend with Columbus as well as with cell phones. At first, Columbus' talk of a new world was ridiculed and rejected. But as the evidence added up, more people jumped on board. Today, there isn't a person on planet earth who still thinks the world is flat.

As cell phones became popular, it was the businessmen and traveling salesmen who would have them in their cars. I was one of the last in my circle of friends to give into the new paradigm. For months, I told everyone, "I don't need a cell phone and I don't want to pay for it," but eventually the wave of change got to me and I, too, gave in. You might be wondering what Christopher Columbus or the birth of the cell phone has to do with changing our priorities as followers of Jesus. In certain ways, the challenge is identical.

A new paradigm means that there's an entirely new way of "doing" life, and that's exactly what Jesus set out to initiate. He didn't come to earth just to die for our sins—He came to establish His kingdom. In the gospel of Mark, the writer records Jesus' first message as He steps on the scene. The words aren't exactly what our 21st century Christianity would expect Him to say. He comes to Galilee and declares, "The time is fulfilled, and the kingdom of God is at hand; repent and believe in the gospel" (Mark 1:15). That's it. That's the core of the message. That's the new paradigm. What about the fact that God loves us and has a wonderful plan for our lives? What about life more abundantly? These things are true, and they are key parts of the message. The kingdom, however, is the central message.

So what is a kingdom? What did Jesus mean that the kingdom of God is at hand? At this point in my own study of the paradigm Jesus introduced, I started looking to define some terms. A kingdom is a realm of rulership. It's a designated area where a certain ruler has absolute authority. For example, the United States is in rulership in North America as far as Canada, and then the rulership changes to the Canadians. If you're in Connecticut for example, then you are in American-ruled territory.

Jesus came to declare that this world belonged to Him. It was under His rulership and He was here to reclaim it. Rulership of this world had been forfeited through sin to Satan and the message of Jesus was that His rulership was back to reclaim His territory, by removing the sin that had first put this earth in Satan's hands. The term "kingdom" speaks of government. Jesus was declaring that His government and authority was supreme—and it was here—and it was advancing.

Next Jesus introduces this idea of the gospel. Most Christians are taught in Sunday school at a young age that the word gospel means "good news." That's true—but the gospel of what? Often when we hear the word "gospel" it's referring to the gospel of salvation. The interesting thing is that Jesus never preached the gospel of salvation. In fact, the three words "gospel of salvation" never appear strung together like that anywhere in my Bible. He did, however, proclaim the gospel of the kingdom, and that is a radically different thing. The good news was not simply that Jesus loves us and died for our sins to save us. The good news was that Jesus came to establish His supreme rule, His kingdom, in our lives and redeem every area of our existence. The purpose for His death on the cross was not to simply pay for our sins. Paying for our sins was a step in the process to get to what He really wanted. The goal was to remove sin so that His Spirit could establish His kingdom in our hearts. This is the gospel that the world desperately needs and the church has tragically misplaced. It's the reality that Christ makes all things new.

The typical "good news" presented in Christianity today is a compartmentalized view of life. We have our time for friends, time for family, time for work or school, time for recreation, and our time for God. We even make tidy lists to prioritize which one comes first or second. I spoke to a friend recently and while we were talking he said, "You know Justin, I need to get better at making God a part of my life." As soon as he said those words, something inside my heart ached. His sentence displayed the false paradigm that blinds and cripples so many of us. Jesus never came to be a part of our lives.

He never came to be on the top of our priority lists. He came instead, to be at the core and center of every thought, action, activity, ambition, and plan. He came to be our life. That is the only option He ever presented for lost humanity.

Jesus doesn't want us to break life into little boxes and then reorder them. The compartmentalized view of our faith produces followers who live one way during "church time" and another way the rest of the time. They see church as an event rather than a lifestyle and this type of paradigm leads to powerless hypocrisy.

Instead, His message was that the kingdom of God must invade every area of life until every aspect of our lives experiences redemption. Family time is His time, work time is His time, and friend time is His time.

Through His teachings, Jesus illustrates this truth in dozens of ways. One way is through yeast. Yep, yeast—the stuff that makes bread rise. I'm not much of a cook, so I had to do a little research to understand the yeast analogy in Matthew 13:33. He tells us that His kingdom is like yeast that is put in some flour. The yeast then spreads throughout all the flour until it overtakes the dough. Bread rises based on how much yeast is put in the dough. God's kingdom is by nature *overtaking* in the human spirit.

There are two qualities about yeast that are worth mentioning. First, it spreads rapidly. Second, when yeast interacts with dough it actually changes the chemical structure of the dough. This is the same as

God's kingdom. When someone experiences the real thing it overtakes their life, becoming the heartbeat behind everything they do. It also changes every part of them in the process. The gospel of the kingdom is an overtaking gospel. It's never a part of life. It is life. It's not just the top of the list because then we can check it off the list and move to the second thing. Instead, it's the center of everything. That's the key.

The good news is that He makes all things new—every area from the inside out. It also means that every moment in life is lived with God. We don't go to church and switch the God button on and then go to work and switch it off. The kingdom of God is meant to be established and ruling in the heart of the believer every moment we are breathing. He's at the center of everything, everywhere, all the time.

The instruction that Jesus gives with the kingdom in Mark 1:15 has two parts. First, He says we have to repent. I know that nobody likes that word anymore, and for good reason. It conjures up thoughts of angry bigots screaming about the end of the world with a home-made sign. But, if Jesus can redeem all of humanity, maybe we can try to redeem that word. To repent literally means to *change your purpose*. It means to leave behind one way of life and fully embrace an entirely different way of life.

This is fundamentally what it means to be a follower of Jesus. He can't be added to our already busy life. He requires repentance—a complete change in purpose. The message of Jesus was to introduce a new way of living and it was all about living for things that are eternal. The trick is that eternal things can't be seen with "non-eternal" eyes and since our human bodies will end up in the ground one day, our natural eyes can't see eternal things. That's why He gives us the second part of the instruction: believe. He's asking us to believe in a kingdom that's built on things that we can't see.

UNDERSTANDING THE NEW PARADIGM

Living in a world full of visual beauty, we naturally begin to assign higher value to pretty things. I love the way Jesus' entire life messes with our "pretty things" paradigm. Think of the things He did. He was God in human flesh and His first strategic move to save mankind was to be born in a barn. His first night on planet earth was spent in a feeding troth between a few goats and donkeys. Today we buy little figurines and make the entire scene pretty, but I'm sure our pretty manger scene is far from reality. If you've ever witnessed the birth of a child, it's beautiful, but it is not clean. I can only imagine the real scene—blood mixed with dirt and hay, surrounded by a few smelly goats. It's cold, it's windy, and the smell of manure fills the air. At this moment, in the mess of real life, the Son of God enters the world in human form. Classic.

He lived a low-profile life for thirty years, and then exploded onto the scene as the most powerful spiritual force in all of Israel. Before long, thousands followed Him, but His radical sermons and illustrations eventually scared many of them away. Then He did something completely unexpected. Jesus allowed Himself to be captured by confused religious zealots and was executed for crimes He didn't commit.

His followers wanted Him to build an army, overthrow Roman oppression, and make Israel the superpower of the world. Instead, Jesus died a criminal's death, but in the invisible world He removed the barrier of sin that had kept all of mankind in slavery since the fall of Adam. He walked out of the grave, proving that the penalty for sin was paid for and purchased for human access to God.

The plan sounds crazy. It sounds like something no one would have ever thought to do, but Jesus understood that if He could gain rulership in the invisible realm, it would spread to every area of reality. Our task, as followers of Christ, is to join Him in His plan of redemption. Jesus was the first anomaly, and He introduced a new paradigm. It wasn't that pretty things were bad, per say. It was that pretty things were defined with a new definition. What is seen no longer holds first place in anything. Instead, the unseen world holds first place in our priorities and our actions.

The Apostle Paul explained the priorities of Jesus to Christians in Corinth when he told them to, "...look not at the things which are seen, but at the things which are not seen; for the things which are seen are temporal, but the things which are not seen are eternal" (2 Cor 4:18).

The secret to the new paradigm lies in what we value. Jesus was able to live for the eternal because He found the way to "look at" unseen things. Remember the story when He stood before Pontius Pilate just before He was sent to be crucified? The Roman leader asked Him if He was the King of the Jews. His answer illustrates the eternal perspective. He replied, "My kingdom is not of this world" (John 18:36). Jesus was plugged into an eternal paradigm. He had changed the basic assumptions of life and while Pilot thought that this man was his prisoner, Jesus knew that the greatest power in existence was the power of an invisible God. The same paradigm, and the same power, is available to us today; we just have to learn to see things differently.

SEEING IT IN SOMEONE ELSE

Have you ever met a Christian who seems to live on a different level? It's almost like they can see something that you can't. I remember one of the first times I interacted with someone like that. It was when I met Harold and Erika in Stuttgart, Germany, and my ministry was doing a series of concerts in the city. Harold and Erika are the parents of four children: Manual, Marin, Dan and Sarah. They live right outside the city of Stuttgart. I stayed in their home on numerous trips to the area and we have since become close friends. The first thing that struck me as different about this family was their genuine closeness. It wasn't the plastic smile "preacher family" closeness that we see all too often. There was something very deep and very genuine.

I remember getting up to go to the bathroom at around six-o-clock one morning while I was staying as a guest in their house. I walked past the living room to find Harold and his oldest son Manuel praying together—But they weren't just praying. They were weeping and singing and worshipping. They were in the presence of God. I thought to myself, "What father and son pray and sing together at six in the morning?" I had never seen anything like it. Then I noticed the way they served others. They gave so selflessly and being around them made me aware of my own selfishness. This family knew that God would reward them for all they gave, and they really believed it. Right away, I realized that they weren't just following "normal" Christian values. They had found something deeper.

One experience with this family revealed to me how God had given them new eyes. It was the day before a concert at the Stuttgart Airport in Germany, where Christians had organized an outreach. A terminal was rented for the event, and the surrounding community was invited to attend. The band that I am a part of was scheduled to play, and I was going to share about Jesus. The day before the concert Harold and Erika asked me and a few of my friends if we would come with them on a special trip. They took us to the outskirts of the airport where there was a German army base. We got out of the car and walked up to the gate of the base.

It was cold and just beginning to rain. I was hoping we wouldn't be outside for too long.

Harold explained why we had come. During World War II, this airport had been a labor camp for Jews. Innocent Jews had been killed on this land. When American troops occupied the area, the American soldiers had responded by brutally torturing and killing the German officers who were running the labor camp. Years later, the airport and the army base were built on the land and the next night, we would hold our concert on that same soil.

Harold and Erika felt like God had asked them to pray for forgiveness for the German people and the injustices towards the Jews, and forgiveness for the American troops for their merciless brutality towards the Germans. They wanted us to pray with them. They sensed that there was a spiritual barrier that we could break through in prayer, and if we would be faithful to pray, God would be faithful to move powerfully the following night. Honestly, I was thinking more about the cold wind and the stinging rain. I was stuck in the world that I could see. They were thinking about a kingdom "not of this world."

We prayed fervently, and the following night God exceeded our wildest expectations. The terminal was packed for the concert and hundreds of people heard the gospel. It was a powerful night that I'll never forget. After the concert, when I was alone, I started to think about the connection between the concerts success and our prayers the day before. I knew that our prayers had affected the outcome of that night. I knew that we had changed something in the invisible realm and saw the results in the visible realm. It was like a light had been turned on. The invisible had collided with the visible and our prayers had shifted the course of events.

This family is an anomaly. They are sensitive enough to the leading of the Holy Spirit that they see the spiritual implications behind physical things and they make decisions based on those spiritual implications. They don't represent the typical Christian family, but they do represent what could be. We can all begin to move mountains and see greater impact in the visible world, when we understand that everything has it's foundation in the invisible world

Jesus came to establish a kingdom, or a realm of rulership, and in order to be a part of the kingdom, we must repent or change our life's purpose. We also need to believe in the supreme impact of the unseen world. Once you've got that foundation, you can take the next step into understanding the priorities of the kingdom.

THE FOUNDATIONAL PRIORITY

Jesus outlined the greatest priority of His kingdom in His most famous sermon to His followers: the Sermon on the Mount. I can only imagine what it would have been like to be there. I wonder if His followers understood the importance of that moment. The Son of God was about to lay out for them the foundational truths that the entire kingdom was to be built upon. In front of thousands of hungry souls, desperate to understand the invisible God, it must have been quite an experience.

Jesus doesn't waste any time. He gets right to the point and starts His message by saying, "Blessed are the poor in spirit for there's is the kingdom of heaven" (Matthew 5:3). Think about this for a second. He's telling us right away the type of person that belongs to the kingdom, but what does it mean to be poor in spirit?

Simply put, it means that everything in your life is defined and submitted to the purposes of God and His rulership. It describes a posture of humility that says that your interests are lost in the interests of the kingdom. Personal interest and kingdom interest can no longer be separated because they are one in the same. You have discovered the secret that all life and joy flow out of Christ so instead of constantly trying to bend your will to His, you've decided to just give your will away and take His will as your own. When you do this, something magical happens—Jesus actually gives you His kingdom. He lets you rule with Him, experience personal redemption through Him, and spread cultural redemption to a dying world.

The poor in spirit look different from the average person. They aren't jockeying for position or trying to get their name in lights. They live a life of absolute consecration because they understand that it is not their kingdom. It's God's kingdom.

No one embodied being poor in spirit better than John the Baptist. I like to study John because I love how weird he was. I imagine him with crooked teeth, scraggly facial hair, and body odor. I don't know if he had any of those, but if he did I'm sure he didn't care too much. He was a man so deeply fixed on the eternal world that things in the natural were seemingly forgotten or at least deemed unimportant. He was the only one to trumpet the message of the kingdom before Jesus, and he knew how kingdom dynamics worked. When Jesus started becoming more popular than John, and many of John's followers started following Jesus, his response is classic. He simply comments, "He must increase, but I must decrease" (John 3:30). This is the heart of those poor in spirit. They don't build their kingdom and they don't seek the world's praise. It was this attitude that allowed John to become a voice to his generation (John 1:23). It's the same attitude that will restore the voice of the church in our generation.

One scholar described the followers of John with words that grabbed my attention. It sounds a lot like the type of people God is looking for today. He wrote that John the Baptist led "a surging crowd of restless eager spirits, sons of a new time, impatient of worn out creeds." Changing priorities and aligning ours with the kingdom starts with being poor in spirit. It means being like John. It means being like the Apostle Paul when he told the church at Corinth that his goal was to give "no cause for offense in anything...but *in everything* commending ourselves as servants of God" (2 Corinthians 6: 3-4 emphasis added). Imagine with me for a minute what this would look like. Imagine the impact it would make on the world to see a community of believers who had given every compartment of their lives over to God—from money, to secret sin, to talents, to giftings! Imagine everything being wrapped up in serving God and increasing His kingdom. No hidden agendas, no jockeying for position, no self-glory. Instead, there would be radical transparency, real accountability, and deep, unwavering consecration. The impact of that type of community would be incredible, and if it began to spread, kingdom priorities could sweep away the stale, obsolete faith that we too often cling to.

THE NEXT STEP

The second piece of God's value system has to do with God's greatest treasure: people. As I'm sure you're aware, we live in a society that doesn't always value people. If you are too old, or too young, or too thin, or too heavy, or too smart, or too stupid, some people may value you less. God does love us because of our external appearance. He puts the highest value on the invisible soul within each of us.

Jesus said, "What will it profit a man if he gains the whole world and forfeits his soul?" (Matthew 16:26). This sentence is a window into God's value system. He is telling us that *one human soul is more valuable than all the "things" of the whole world put together.* Read that last sentence again—let it sink in for a second. If you traded your soul for all the money and power and pleasure that this world has to offer, you would be getting ripped off. The soul is literally the most valuable thing on planet earth.

Think of it now from God's perspective. He created the human race and gave us the freedom to obey Him or reject Him. The first humans decided to disobey Him, and this produced a sinful nature in every person because every person came from the first two. Something shifted on the inside of Adam when he disobeyed. His nature became sinful and he passed that nature on to all his children. The only way to make it right between God and man was for the full penalty of sin to be paid for. However, the only thing that held that kind of eternal value was the sacrifice of a perfect person in the place of an imperfect race. This perfect person could pay the penalty owed to God, and begin a new race of people with a godly nature.

The only problem was that there were no perfect people—unless God himself decided to take on human flesh and supernaturally be born to a virgin. This way He wouldn't inherit Adam's imperfect nature. If God did this, which of course would be crazy, He could die for the sins of the human race and His death could pay our debt in full. Once our debt was paid, death couldn't hold Him anymore. He could conquer death and be resurrected from the dead.

But is this possession that valuable? Is one human soul so valuable that the God of the universe would limit Himself to a human form and then die just to have us back in His possession? Jesus' life and death proved that the human soul is that valuable, and if we are to live by His priorities, our lives must reflect that same value system. The elderly person, the disabled person, the minority, the unattractive person—everyone that the world would consider less valuable holds immeasurable eternal value in the eyes of God. Since God designed this whole world and puts that much value on the human soul, it has to be the most valuable thing on the planet.

How should this idea of the value of one soul affect our daily lives? It is an entirely new paradigm. It's like Columbus and his new map of the world. It changes everything.

After I had encountered God as a teenager, I decided to read the New Testament and do what it said. That may sound obvious and simple, but I wanted to do everything it said. I wanted to try it out and see what would happen. This hunger led me to countless adventures on the green downtown with a few of my friends. We weren't trained ministers. In fact, looking back we may have done more harm than good in some cases. But our hearts were honest and hungry to see God move and He never let us down. One day, as I walked across the green I saw a man lying in a pile of newspapers. He was sleeping and it was clear that he was homeless. Something inside me told me to go over and talk to him. After a few minutes of debate in my mind, I decided to swallow my fear and timidity and go over to him.

The man slowly woke up and I asked him if he wanted help. He looked a little confused. I'd probably be confused too if I were in his position and a seventeen-year-old kid was waking me up. I told him, "I want to help you. Do you want to come with me?" The man finally sat up and looked at me. I introduced myself and told him about how Jesus had changed my life. I wanted to help him any way I could. I'm sure that I wasn't the first Jesus do-gooder he had encountered but he wasn't really in a picky mood.

He said he needed some food and a shower. I told him to hop in my jeep. Understand I wasn't an educated social activist trying to alleviate homelessness in America. I was a teenage kid who was gripped with the idea that God deeply valued this man's life and in that moment, God was asking me to intervene. So, we cruised in my jeep back to my friend's house. Four teenage kids and a sixty five-year-old homeless man driving down the road in a Jeep Wrangler with the top down on a sunny summer afternoon—it made for an incredible memory.

I got to know Harold pretty well that day. Within a few hours, he had showered, shaved, and looked good. The more we talked, the more God started to change my heart and open my eyes. He wasn't a homeless guy with a beard. He wasn't a distant being. In fact, he wasn't so different from me. He was somebody's husband and somebody's father. He had a mom and a dad and a story. He was a person.

After Harold had showered, shaved, and gotten a bite to eat, the four of us asked if we could pray with him. He quickly agreed. Almost immediately, the atmosphere in the room started to change. A warmth and an electricity started filling the room and the five of us there all sensed it. After the prayer, Harold looked up with tears in his eyes and said, "I don't know what you kids did to me, but I feel totally different." We all smiled. He had just been introduced to the Holy Spirit.

The next day Harold came to church with us and publicly made Jesus the king of his life. It was an historic moment. An elderly man in borrowed clothes had come to the end of his rope and in front of nearly five hundred people, humbly admitted his need for this great God. It was beautiful.

Weeks went by and then months and Harold and I lost touch. It wasn't until a few years later that I saw him again. I was leading worship at a church that was hosting our band. As I started to sing a song, I looked out into the congregation and to my surprise, I saw Harold standing next to a Christian friend who had brought him to church. He was growing, and with the help of some Christians who were devoted to helping him grow, He was breaking free from his past.

Life is inherently messy. It's like that manger where Jesus was born. I can still remember the funny smell Harold brought into my Jeep that lingered for days. Things just aren't as clean and picturesque as we'd like them to be, but God's eternal love for humanity inspired Jesus to embrace and even become a part of our mess. As we allow His kingdom to establish a foundation in our hearts, we can learn to embrace the mess too. Selfishness and self-centered living have no place in the kingdom. If one soul is more valuable than all the things of the world combined, then I want to give my life to influence people towards Jesus and away from lies. Why would I ever spend my life collecting pretty things and trying to get the newest toys when I could be influencing the destinies of eternal souls?

STEP THREE

As soon as we submit our will to God and realize that people are the most valuable thing on the planet, the third part of this new set of priorities has to do with our view of eternity. I keep mentioning an "eternal perspective," but what does it mean to see things in the light of eternity? Simply put, it means to realize that after this life, there is a next life. The next life won't have a short time span like this one. We won't be there for seventy years of eighty-three years, or fifty years. In the next life, we will be there forever.

Since this life is short, and the next life is forever, it makes sense to spend our time now focused on how our actions will affect the next life. But where do we go after this life? The scripture describes two very specific places, and tragically, for many of us these places are just distant ideas. Their reality hasn't affected the way we live. That needs to change.

The first place is Heaven. Heaven isn't a place for fat babies with wings and harps. It's a literal place where those who have trusted in Jesus Christ will go when they die. Our physical bodies will stay on this planet and eventually decompose (since everything that is visible is temporary) and our spiritual person will go to Heaven. Heaven is described in many different places in the Bible, and Jesus assured us that He will prepare a place for all of His followers in Heaven (John 14:1-6). As a follower of Jesus, I don't need to be afraid of dying. Although a lot about death is mysterious, I can be sure that God will be there with me on the other side. I remember when I first discovered the peace that comes with trusting in Jesus for my eternal salvation. He told His followers that if we trust fully in Him, we will have eternal life (John 3:15-18). Scripture describes Heaven as a place of peace, and healing, and closeness to God. It's a place where the barriers between us and God are completely gone. We are with Him.

I think it's important for followers of Jesus to look forward to heaven. If we live our lives always scared of dying then we prove that we don't really believe what we claim. I can't even imagine what it will be like to look at God face to face, but we will in Heaven. What if there are new colors that don't exist on this earth and new sounds that we've never heard? What will it be like to talk with the saints of old and walk side by side with Jesus and see the scars on His hands? It will be glorious.

The second place described in scripture is Hell. This idea of Hell is something that most Christians don't spend much time thinking about. I know plenty of people who think that Hitler and Saddam Hussein are the only two people in Hell. It violates something inside of us to think that a loving God would allow "good" people to go to a place of torment for eternity. So instead of dealing with this reality of Hell, many of us have decided to ignore it.

The paradigm that Jesus introduced to the world didn't dodge the Hell issue. In fact, it was this reality of Hell that moved Jesus so deeply that He was willing to give His life to save us from it. The Bible tells us that those who do not know God and those who do not obey the gospel of the Lord Jesus will pay the penalty of eternal destruction (2 Thessalonians 1: 7-10). So it's those who don't obey and those who don't know Him. That's pretty clear and it makes most of us pretty uncomfortable. We don't want to read that verse. We don't want to think about it.

If we really want to see with new eyes, then we must have the courage to look at this truth until it changes us on the inside. Hell is described as a place of great physical pain (Luke 16:24). Think of the last time you experienced an intense amount of pain. I remember when I was a little kid and I accidentally sliced off a chunk of my thumb with my pocketknife. The doctor stitched my thumb back together, but I could feel every stitch. No amount of painkiller seemed to relieve the pain. If Hell is a place of great pain, then my throbbing thumb is just a small glimpse into Hell.

The Bible tells us that there will be weeping and wailing (Matthew 8:11-12). When I read that, I think of the last time I heard someone really weep. When someone is weeping, it grabs the heart of those who hear it. Even if we don't know the person, we begin to hurt for them. I can be watching a movie or walking down the street but if I hear someone weeping, I'm immediately alarmed and concerned. Weeping carries a certain degree of hopelessness and there is nothing more hopeless than the reality of Hell.

Hell is also a place of darkness. Imagine for a moment the last time you were in a room that was pitch black. Imagine being stuck in that room for an hour, or three hours, or an entire day. It wouldn't be long before you began to panic. Then you realize that there was no way out of that room—ever.

When I was in college, I painted houses part-time to make some extra cash. One time I worked for a very nice woman who was dying of a terminal illness. She was in her sixties, and she stayed in her bedroom all day hooked up to a breathing machine while we painted her house. The woman was completely conscious, but the doctor's report was not optimistic. I tried to stay focused on the job, but my heart was melting inside of me for her. I knew that she would be walking into the next life soon, and I didn't know where she stood with God. I finally built up the courage to talk with her.

I sparked a conversation with her and tried to guide it gently towards God. As I approached the topic of Jesus, the lady smiled and said to me, "Honey, since I was a little girl I was raised in a Jewish home and taught to believe that Jesus was not the Son of God. I don't want to change that now." We talked for a few more minutes and I realized that she was not interested in hearing about Jesus. Later that day, we finished the paint job at her house, packed up our gear, and said goodbye. I got in my car, started driving home, and then something came over me.

My heart broke for this woman and I began to weep uncontrollably. I could see how much God loved her and how much He wanted to save her. I could also see that she was unwilling to be saved. I pulled my car over to the side of the road and my heart became like wax. I sat there and wept for this woman who I didn't even know. I can't remember her name and I never saw her again, but that day God let me feel His heartbeat. He let me see with His eyes. The reality of Hell had gripped my heart and messed up my plans. I wasn't just reading about it in a religious book. I was looking its reality in the face and allowing it to shake me. The truth is, until it really shakes you on the inside, you can't live for eternity, and you won't be able to see it.

The Bible tells us that God wants all people to be saved and come to the knowledge of the truth (1 Timothy 2:3-4). He also tells us that He has given us the choice to follow Him or to reject Him (Deuteronomy 30:19). Satan wants to blind the eyes of the unbelieving and keep them in a place of unbelief (2 Corinthians 4:4). That day as we left the house, my eyes were opened to the eternal battle that rages for souls. I didn't want to see that woman go to Hell. I didn't want to reach the joy of heaven and realize that she was trapped in darkness for eternity.

These thoughts about Hell are uncomfortable. Some people might call them alarmist. It doesn't matter what we call them. It's real. The truth is that the greatest emergency facing this generation is not drugs or immorality or humanism. The greatest emergency is that millions of people do not know God and do not obey the gospel. This makes them candidates for Hell. This reality needs to grip our hearts and move us to do something. How can I spend hours with a friend talking about football and music when I know that they are on the road to hell? How can I ignore my responsibility to share God's love and grace?

STEP FOUR

There is a fourth step to getting our priorities straight and this one has to do with the way we view our time. Where we spend our time needs to reflect the previous three priorities. In other words, our time management will be the proof that we actually are practicing a kingdom worldview. If we are agreeing with these priorities in our heads but not actually designating time to practice them, then our growth in God can go no further. Time will always tell.

A few years ago, I had the opportunity to take a three-week long ministry trip to Europe. We visited four countries and ministered nineteen times in twenty days. It was intense. About halfway through the trip we traveled to the Netherlands for a few days of ministry. On our last day in the Netherlands, we decided to take the train into Amsterdam and play some music in the square downtown. Our hope was to draw a crowd and have an opportunity to share our faith. It turned out to be a night that I will never forget.

Amsterdam is like no other place I've ever been. With legalized prostitution and drug use, it's a place where most Christians feel a little uncomfortable. It was a wild scene—a bunch of Christian kids in downtown Amsterdam singing about Jesus. People didn't know what to do with us. We played a few songs and some people gathered around to listen. A group of Chinese tourists took pictures and a few drunk guys tried to join the festivities. After a couple songs, our team broke into small groups and started sharing with those who had gathered. As I packed up my guitar, a girl about my age introduced herself. Her name was Anna.

Anna was from Sylvania. She had graduated from school and had no idea what she wanted to do with her life. So instead of getting some job that she hated, Anna decided to come to Amsterdam and hopefully "find herself." She happened to be walking by and heard us singing and talking about Jesus and something inside her felt drawn to us. As we started to talk, I could tell that God was drawing Anna. She was hungry to find Him, but she had no idea that Jesus was the one she was looking for. The conversation continued, and I felt compelled to tell her clearly. "Anna, Jesus is the person you've been looking for. He needs to fill that hole in your life." She seemed opened to the idea, but a little skeptical.

My discussion with Anna went on for a while and my friend Lindsey joined the conversation. She asked us about our music group and why we were in Amsterdam. I told her about our trip and the places we had been. Then she asked me where we would be going next. We were leaving for Germany the next morning. As I said that, I heard Lindsey chime in, "Yeah, you should come with us to Germany."

As soon as she said those words, my blood froze. We didn't even know this girl. She wasn't a Christian. We couldn't take her with us! I thought about all the important Christian stuff we had to do in Germany. We had to meet with pastors, go to prayer meetings, and set up for events. What would we do with this unsaved Sylvanian girl if she came with us?

My thoughts raced around in my head as I considered how inconvenient and disruptive this could be. I opened my mouth looking for the right words to defuse this bomb and I found myself saying, "Yeah, you should come with us!" Anna told us she would consider it, and if she decided to come, she would meet us at the train station at nine in the morning the next day. We said goodbye and headed back to where we were staying.

On the ride back that night, I battled with my thoughts. I didn't want to mess up our agenda. Truthfully, I hadn't surrendered my time fully to God. I fought through these feelings and we prayed that God would speak to Anna. The next morning, we got to the train station at nine-o-clock and she wasn't there. We walked around the station. We waited for her. She wasn't there. Finally, we decided to board the train and leave for Germany. As we did, Anna came running through the station! She told as that the city transportation had gone on strike and she had walked to the train station. Within minutes, we were on our way to Germany with one extra passenger!

The next few days were wild. Anna came with us to Christian leadership meetings, prayer walks, and even sat through planning meetings. There were times when it was awkward, but God had a bigger plan. Finally, a few days into the ministry in Germany, after dinner one night Anna began to talk with a woman in our group about her relationship with God. A few of us started praying in another room for Anna to receive Christ. As we cried out to God, someone on our team came in and told us that Anna had just surrendered her heart to Jesus! The joy of that moment is indescribable. The eternity of this one girl had been changed because we had taken a risk and decided to do something that was inconvenient.

My experience with Anna changed my perspective. It was a paradigm shift in my life. I knew that I needed to surrender every area to God and that meant that my agenda belonged to Him. I began to see the value of one life and how much God cares for every individual. I started to understand that life must be lived with eternity in mind and I needed to seize the moment.

Our twenty-day trip to Europe was powerful and we played a lot of concerts and ministered to a lot of people. God moved in so many special ways. There was something, however, that was particularly special about this experience with Anna. There were no lights and no crowds. There was no financial reward. It represents, for me, the substance of real Christianity. The experience with Anna taught me to apply these other priority shifts in a practical way, and it also taught me that applying God's priorities will often mess up my schedule.

How does God view this idea of time, and how are we supposed to use the time we have? I think that the first mistake we make is that we take time for granted. We act like we'll be around forever, and we can control what happens tomorrow. Instead of taking our time for granted, God wants us to live with the realization that this life is like a vapor. One minute you can see it, then the next minute it's gone (James 4:13-

16). None of us can control tomorrow, so we must seize the moment and live it to its fullest.

Think for a minute about the last three "priority shifts" that have been described. First, completely surrendering to God, second, viewing people as the most valuable treasure on earth, and third, allowing eternity to effect the way that we live every day. Now think of each of those priorities through the truth that our life is a vapor.

If you're like me, just thinking about this stuff will inject urgency into your veins and cause you to want to make the most of your time. This is exactly what God is looking to accomplish in us (Ephesians 5: 15-17). He's not trying to make us into lunatics who run around and try to make things happen in our own efforts. We can't save people, only He can, but we can be attentive, submitted and prepared. We can live every day with our time surrendered to God, our time focused on other people, and our time working to accomplish eternal results.

Sin becomes even more repelling because it distracts us from our eternal work. Scheduling and planning are important, and I believe that we should prayerfully plan our time, but this needs to be balanced with being led by the Holy Spirit moment by moment. We can't be lazy or inactive. We must seize the day.

Five hundred years ago, Christopher Columbus stood before the rulers of Spain and introduced a new paradigm. I'm sure people laughed at him. I'm sure there were moments when he questioned himself and felt like a failure. But in the end, Columbus had found a better map.

Today, in a church that has lost her voice, we are in desperate need of a better map. The version of Christianity that makes God a part of our Sunday routines but never invades our lives simply does not work. It does not bring real life change. We need to see the substance of Christianity in action. People who model the priorities of Heaven—that is what the world is waiting for.

Chapter 3
FINDING THE REAL YOU

Everyone who has ever lived on a college campus has at least three or four unforgettable stories about their college roommates. Years after graduation, you'll find yourself sitting around a coffee table swapping your tall tales about crazy roommates and crazy experiences. My stories began when I moved into Schwartz Hall, room 501 with three other students. Kofi, Ben, and Prince soon became three of my closest friends.

From the first day we moved in together anyone could see that we had come from different worlds. Kofi was the running back for the university football team. He's made of pure muscle, and he has more style in one outfit than most people do in their entire wardrobe. He's black, he likes rap music, and he grew up in the city. Kofi was almost a legend on campus. Having gone to high school not far from the university, he had dominated high school football in previous years.

Ben was from down south. He was a wide receiver for the football team and had transferred from a school in North Carolina to play football in Connecticut. He's over six feet tall, listened to country music and has a smile that lights up a room. Ben is one of those people who everyone loves to be around. His subtle southern accent and friendly personality make him stand out in a crowd.

Prince was the quiet type. His family was from India and he spoke with an Indian accent. He often worked on his computer, and bought more food for our room than everyone else combined. Prince is one of the most thoughtful guys I've ever met. He'd think of other people all the time and do little things to express his thoughtfulness.

Then there was me. I'm a skinny white kid who plays guitar in a band. I didn't play football, didn't like rap or country music, and didn't know the first thing about India. There was only one thing that linked the four of us together, but that one thing proved to be far stronger than the color of our skin, the style of our clothes or the music on our ipods. Every one of us had experienced the power and love of Jesus in a way that had transformed our lives. For me, it happened as a young-teenager. For Kofi and Ben, it happened when they got to college. Regardless of when it happened, our four hearts were tied together in the pursuit of following Jesus and figuring out who we were supposed to be. And on a campus of over 12,000 students, most of whom knew nothing about following Jesus, we needed each other. Our room was transformed into an epicenter of spiritual growth and hunger for God.

Then it happened. It was in all other respects a normal morning and I had just woken up. Kofi and Prince had already left for the day and Ben wasn't in bed. He was standing by the window deep in thought. I wasn't sure if he was upset or happy so I walked over to him and asked what was going on. He looked at me and said, "Justin, I think I heard God." I asked him what he meant. He explained, "This morning I woke up and I had heard a voice in a dream. It sounded like it was coming from a radio in the dream, but I think God is trying to speak to me. I keep hearing it again and again in my head."

I could tell from the way Ben was sharing with me that he wasn't joking around. He had really heard God's voice. God had walked into our bedroom and spoken to Ben. Somehow, I had managed to sleep through it. So I asked him the only question worth asking. "What did God say?" Ben started to speak, then hesitated, then started again. "See, it's kind of weird. He told me, 'Just because you know how you are, doesn't mean you know who you are.'"

It was like an atomic bomb went off in the room. There was something about the statement that was simple, but really profound at the same time. It had that funny "God signature." *Just because you know how you are, doesn't mean you know who you are.* We spent the day thinking about the statement and what God was trying to say to us. Ultimately, it came down to one word: identity. This was God's way of forcing Ben to take a fresh look at his identity. Ben had traveled hundreds of miles, left his family and his girlfriend in North Carolina and moved to Connecticut to play football. He had suffered an injury at the beginning of the season and had been sitting on the bench. During this time, Ben also got serious about his relationship with God and he now found himself at a crossroads. All his life he had been known as "Ben the football player." If God was taking football out of his life, then who was he? He wasn't just supposed to be "Ben the Christian," was he?

Everything rises and falls on identity. It seems that when God decides to break into our world and speak audibly, He almost always goes right for this issue of identity. When Jesus was being baptized by John the Baptist and the crowd heard an audible voice from Heaven, the voice didn't say, "I love you." It didn't say, "Everyone needs to follow this Jesus guy." The voice simply dealt with Jesus' identity. It said, "This is my beloved Son, in whom I am well pleased" (Matthew

3:17). Ben had made the mistake that we all make. He had found his identity through what he did or "how he was" rather than through "who he was." He thought he was a football player, but that was just something he did.

Who are you? Do you define yourself through a hobby or a talent? Growing up in your family were you the jock, or the computer geek, or the artist? Were you the musician, or the straight "A" student, or the class clown? These are all different traits, but they do not get to the core of who you are.

Maybe you come from a family that takes a lot of pride in your race or ethnicity. Maybe you find your identity in the fact that you're white, or black or Hispanic. It could be that you're proud to be Irish or Italian or Portuguese. It's not wrong to hold onto your family heritage, but there is a higher, more eternal view of your identity. In Heaven, there is no white, black, Irish or Chinese. The Bible goes right to the root of the tree and says that our true citizenship is in Heaven (Philippians 3:20). Again, Jesus never once takes His eyes off the primary message. He came to announce a kingdom.

Many of us like to define ourselves through our occupations. If you begin dating someone and they take you to meet their parents, the first question the parents will ask is, "So, what do you do for a living?" Are you a doctor, or a teacher, or a construction worker, or a student? Your occupation might be how you make money, but it is not who you are. We tend to think of ourselves a certain way because we make a certain amount of money, or drive a certain type of car, or live in a certain part of town. In the eyes of Jesus, these things don't mean much and if I am committed to living for His kingdom, why should they mean much to me?

Growing up, there was one kid in my neighborhood who was much cooler than the rest of us. His name was Sebastian. He was three or four years older than all the other kids. He was a really good skateboarder and soccer player. All the girls liked him. As soon as I figured out that Sebastian was the coolest, I decided to do all the things that he did. He liked the old 80's band Guns and Roses, so I liked them too. He skateboarded, so I went out and bought a skateboard. He wore certain clothes, so I tried to wear the same type of clothes. The only problem was that I was a complete phony. I have very little coordination with my feet so I quickly found out that skateboarding and soccer didn't come easy. It wasn't long before I became even less cool for trying to be like Sebastian.

Why do we do these things? Why do we copy other people? In a culture that tells me to "be myself," my problem was that I didn't know who "myself" was and when I gave my life to Jesus, I took all of my insecurities and backwards thinking with me. I had to learn that living for another world meant leaving behind my false perceptions of identity and finding my identity through Jesus. I'll be the first to say, the process can be scary.

I love the movie *Hook* with Robin Williams. In the movie, Robin Williams plays Peter Pan who left Neverland and grew up to become a ruthless, selfish businessman in the real world. In the process, Peter forgets that he used to be the brave and courageous leader of the lost boys. He's forced to travel back to Neverland when his kids are kidnapped by Captain Hook. The whole movie is the story of Peter rediscovering his true identity.

At first, he doesn't even believe that he's Peter Pan. Tinker Bell knows that the only way for Peter to rescue his kids is for him to remember. She brings him to familiar places throughout Neverland to jog his memory and half way through the movie, Peter finally rediscovers his lost identity. There's this one scene when Peter goes before the lost boys and tries to convince them that he really is their old leader. No one believes him—except this one little kid. The boy grabs Peters face and starts stretching his skin. Finally, he catches a glimpse of the Peter Pan he used to know. The boy exclaims, "There's Peter!" One by one, the other boys can see the young Peter in the body of this full grown man. One by one, they affirm his identity.

In the kingdom of God, who you are determines how far you can go. Peter Pan couldn't fly until he knew that he was Peter Pan. Like Peter, the "real you" is buried under all of your false concepts of who you are and we have to set aside the old definitions before we can discover the real definition.

Imagine for a moment that you are no longer the jock, the businessman, or the skateboarder. You may know how you are, but now it's time to figure out who you are.

A CHILD OF GOD

The first clue to discovering your identity begins with where you came from. Your physical body came from your parents. Their genes were blended in a unique way and it resulted in you. Your spirit, however, didn't come from your parents. It was born the day that you accepted Christ as your savior and received His Spirit into your heart. That day, your spirit was "made alive" and you were adopted into God's spiritual family. Your physical body only lasts for one lifetime on this earth, but your spiritual identity lasts forever. This means that when it really comes down to finding the real you, it makes sense to define yourself by the part of you that lasts forever, rather than by the part of you that only lasts for your life on this earth. Your spirit is the real you.

Scripture tells us that when we join ourselves to Jesus, our spirit and His spirit are joined together (1 Cor 6:17). Just like when two people are married, they become "one person," when we are joined to God, we become one with Him. Because of this coming together, we've been given the right to be called children of God (John 1:12) and being a child of God comes with certain privileges. The Father sees you the same way that He sees Jesus and you can come as close to God the Father as Jesus can. Think about that fact for a second. Let that truth push through all the unworthiness and shame that tries to block you. When God looks at you, He sees the perfection of Jesus.

Since you have become united with Jesus Christ by accepting Him into your heart, all the love, acceptance, power, and glory that the Father has given to Jesus—Jesus has given to you! The Bible doesn't say that every person on planet earth is a child of God. It says that all of those who receive Christ have become God's children (John 1:12). My real identity begins with where I came from. Since my spirit and Jesus' spirit have become one, and He came from heaven, I came from heaven too. This makes me a citizen of heaven. This is where my spirit calls home and even though I can't see it, it's more real than the world around me.

Are you confused yet? I know it's taken me a long time to wrap my brain around this idea of being God's son. How could God view me the same way He views Jesus? Why would He choose to do that?

God's love is foreign. It's "other." It's too big, and too perfect, and too unconditional for our finite minds to fully grasp. It doesn't fit into our human way of thinking. I used to think of God's love like the perfect version of my love, but that is not true. It's not human love perfected to the hundredth degree. His love is something all together different than what the human mind can even calculate. That's how He can love us in spite of our failures and sins.

In Hosea, chapter 11 God explains His undying love for His people, even though they rebel against Him. He tells them that, "My heart is turned over within Me" and "All My compassions are kindled." His love is so huge and His heart breaks as He experiences their rejection. God mentions how He "taught them to walk." Like a Father who's son has run away from home, God's heart turns within Him when we are not close to Him. He is the perfect loving Father and we are the object of His affection. We are His treasure and our acceptance of Christ has made us sons and daughters. Think about that! A child of God. If our imperfect parents can love us, how much more our perfect Father! If I would never abandon my son on earth, how much more will God never abandon me!

The athlete has an identity crisis as soon as he can no longer play his sport. The businessman has an identity crisis as soon as his business fails. But the child of God is not shaken. He has found something solid.

SONS AND DAUGHTERS

I went through a time in my life where my heart was desperately crying out for a father. I love my earthly father very much and he loves me, but something deep inside me was looking for a greater understanding of my identity. My parents were divorced as a kid, and my dad always stayed in the picture, but I still found within myself this longing for a father to really lead me. My first reaction was to try to find my identity in other godly people. I ended up going to this church service where a well-known preacher was talking about spiritual fathers and mothers. At the end of the service, the preacher asked anyone who wanted prayer to come forward. My heart almost exploded inside of me. I thought to myself, "Finally I'm going to be healed from this deep wound I don't even understand."

I ran up front and waited patiently for prayer. Time passed, and still the famous preacher didn't get to me. Finally, after almost everyone else had received prayer, I got his attention. I'll never forget the moment. I was ready for breakthrough. I was full of faith. I was believing that I would be healed from my woundedness through the prayers of this man of God. The famous preacher looked at me, and smiled. He said, "Young man I think my ministry tonight is done. I'm exhausted and I feel that it's time for me to call it a night. God bless you." He patted my shoulder, walked by me to grab his coat and headed for his hotel. I stood there, like a kid who's lost his parents at a playground.

I was stunned. I had mustered the courage to respond for prayer and open this wound, and my hopes of healing had just left for the hotel. Finally, I went back to my seat, buried my head in my hands, and wept. Hundreds of people around me were singing and enjoying the service, and I was sitting in the back crying. I felt like an orphan. I wanted so badly to know the deep love and guidance of a spiritual father. Then, I heard God's quiet whisper in the deepest part of my heart. He simply said, "What you are looking for can only be found in Me. I'm your Father. I'm proud of you."

That was my moment. That's when I got it. For the first time in my life, my identity had a foundation. Above all else, I was a child of God. I was one of His sons and regardless of my accomplishments or earthly stature, my identity was secure. I didn't need to win the world's approval and I didn't need to rest in the stability of others. I had found my dad.

Why does God call Himself Father? He could have called Himself mother, uncle, or cousin. God isn't male or female, but still Jesus taught us to pray, "Our Father." Why? I believe it's because God designed human beings with a need that only a father can fulfill. I'm not trying to downplay the need for moms. They are incredibly important. Still there is a need in the heart of every person that only God the Father can meet. Though it's different for men and women, both need their Father to affirm their identity. When we are affirmed by our Father, we have the support and the security that we need to take on the world.

MADE CLEAN

It's important to know that you are a child of God, and that will get you started, but there's more to this identity thing. I remember the first time I stumbled over 1 Corinthians 1:8. It says that God will confirm me to the end, *blameless*. I thought to myself, "Well that can't be right." I've committed plenty of sins and I believe that

God has forgiven me, but that doesn't make me blameless does it? Scripture goes on to tell us that God has, "forgiven us all our transgressions" (Col 2:13), and that He, "canceled out the certificate of debt consisting of decrees against us" (Col 2:14). When I first read this stuff I couldn't handle it. What does God mean with this type of language?

The Apostle Paul writes to the Roman church that believers are "justified as a gift" (Rom 3:24) and John tells us that, "the blood of Jesus cleanses us from all sin" (1 John 1:7). The day Jesus died on the cross, His blood became the perfect substitute for every sin in my past and every sin in my future. I am completely blameless in the eyes of God. I'm completely clean. The bigger problem that we face is that most of us live our lives acting like we're still dirty. We just don't feel clean.

A few years ago, just days after Hurricane Katrina hit Louisiana and Mississippi, I got a phone call from my father-in-law. He told me that he was going to Mississippi to help the victims of the hurricane and asked if I wanted to come. A couple days later, me and a number of my friends packed into an RV and drove down. When we got there, the rescue teams put us right to work. We went into the victims homes and dug through the thick Mississippi mud to try and recover possessions and clear doorways. By the time the sun went down, we were covered from head to toe in the mud. We went back to our RV in desperate need of a shower.

I found out quickly that it's difficult to do anything when you're that dirty. I couldn't eat. I couldn't sleep. I couldn't even relax. My sweat had mixed with the mud and left me feeling completely disgusting. Then, in the midst of our desperation, one of my friends had an idea. He took two of the Poland Spring water jugs that were being brought in on crates for fresh drinking water, and climbed to the top of a nearby building. He stripped down to his underwear and dumped those water jugs over his head. Within seconds, all the guys grabbed two jugs of our own and headed for the building. I'll never forget looking out over the ravaged landscape as the sun set in Biloxi, Mississippi. We soaped up, smiled wide, and dumped those jugs over our heads. It was glorious. I left the roof of that building feeling cleaner than I've ever felt in my life.

Physical realities often help give us a footing with spiritual truths. We all know what it feels like to come home from a project feeling dirty and in need of a shower, and we all know that hanging around in those dirty clothes gets old pretty fast. We would never do it in the physical, but most Christians get used to walking around in spiritual filth when God has declared us blameless. This is exactly the attitude that Satan and demonic forces want believers to have. For many of us, it isn't pride, lust or greed that keeps us from doing great things for God. It's shame. We are plagued with guilt from our past failures and we are convinced that God would never use someone like us.

The day I realized that Jesus had shed His blood to make me completely clean was the day that I washed off the mud. But it does not stop there. I've found that I must daily renew my thinking and put my faith in God's righteousness rather than my own. As a child of God, I don't have to walk around feeling like a failure. There is a place for us in Christ where we are completely free from the guilt of our past sin, and that's where I want to live.

Finding the real you means finding God's view of you. Throughout the New Testament, God tells us again and again that we can't come to Him by our own righteousness. The gift of God is not simply that He washes us off. It's that He gives us the righteousness of Jesus as a free gift. We have to remove our own righteousness. We have to get rid of the idea that we can work our way to God. We have to completely reject the idea that we've been "good enough" today, so God will hear our prayers. As followers of Jesus, we've been given a free gift. That gift is the perfect righteousness of Jesus. Only when I accept it can I interact with God the way that He designed me to interact with Him. The secret to living life free from sin starts with believing in the cleansing power of the cross.

FREE AT LAST

I once heard a story about the great escape artist Harry Houdini. It was said that Houdini could wiggle his way out of the strongest chains and figure out a way to unlock any lock. He was a master. So, one day a man came to Houdini and challenged the master's ability. He locked Houdini in a jail cell, tied him up with the thickest chains, and gave him only a few minutes to escape the cell. As the clock began to tick, Houdini quickly found a way out of the chains. He jumped to his feet and began working on the jail cell door. Seconds passed and Houdini began to sweat. Soon minutes had gone by. Finally, there were only a few seconds left on the timer and Houdini still hadn't been able to figure out the lock on the door. He pushed and prodded but he just couldn't get it.

As time expired, Houdini leaned his head up against the bars. He had been defeated. The jail cell door was too difficult for him. The man who had challenged him walked up to the door, put his hand on the handle, and pressed it down. The door slowly creaked open. Harry Houdini realized that he had been fooled, and that the jail cell door was never locked. All that time he was trying to pick a lock that didn't exist!

When I first gave my life to Jesus, I quickly realized that I had some sinful areas that I couldn't control. I asked other Christians about it and they would often say something like, "Well, you'll always struggle, and everyone falls sometimes." That answer didn't sit right with me. I asked myself, "Why would God go through all this trouble to forgive my sins, call me his child, and make me clean, and then just leave me powerless to overcome sinful habits in my life?"

For a while, I tried to fight against these sinful habits on my own. I failed. Then I realized that I had been like Houdini. I was trying to unlock a door that had been unlocked for me. I was living in a jail cell, a slave to my sinful habits, when God had already unlocked the door. In order for me to be free, I had to put my faith in the fact that God had freed me. As the Apostle Paul puts it, I had to consider myself to be dead to sin (Rom 6:11).

Scripture tells us that our body of sin was crucified with Christ. Just as we can know our identity as children of God because we are one with Jesus, we can also find our victory over sinful habits because we are one with Jesus. In the eyes of our Father, we are united with Jesus in our spirit, and when Jesus died on the cross, our old sinful nature died with Him (Rom 6:6). Because Jesus rose from the grave, we can live in victory over sin. Sin itself isn't dead. It's still roaming around trying to pull Christians into its jail cell. But our sinful nature is dead when we put our faith in God's perspective rather than our own.

We are instructed not to let sin reign in our bodies (Rom 6:12). I don't believe in a God who forgives His children but then leaves them as slaves. We can be free from sin. If we do fall, we don't need to stay far from God. We can run to Him, receive His forgiveness and continue to push ahead. Day by day, God will show us the way out of the jail.

If we believe and hold to God's truth, our sinful nature can be done away with (Rom 6:6). The words that the Apostle Paul uses to describe this can also be translated as "rendered powerless." It literally means, "To tear something down until it's completely idle." That description makes me think of a National Geographic clip where an alligator catches a deer or an antelope and drags it to the bottom of the sea. The animal fights and kicks for a while, but eventually it is rendered powerless against the alligator. If you and I learn to walk in faith and believe God for His power over sin, we can wrestle every temptation down to the floor and render it powerless. God promises to never allow us to be tempted beyond what we are able, and provide a way of escape so that we can endure temptation (1 Cor 10:13). He tells us that He will strengthen us and protect us from the enemy (2 Thes 3:3). I can't tell you how many times I've run to those promises in moments of temptation. I still run to them. These promises hold the power to be free from sinful habits.

As long as we see ourselves as slaves in a jail cell, we will live as slaves in a jail cell. It's only when we have new eyes that we begin to realize that God didn't save us to be slaves. He saved us to be free. Perfection is not a destination. It's a daily journey. Every day we can draw closer to God and He can reveal more of the sin that needs to be removed. Every day we can experience more of His freedom, and in the process, discover our own true identity. Remember, the gospel of the kingdom is that He came to make all things new, even our secret failures. The new life begins as we come into the light and surrender these things to Him.

PARTNER'S WITH GOD

Years ago, I was an intern for a social service agency in Connecticut. One day, I was asked to go to court for one of our clients with my supervisor. I was excited about the opportunity. I wanted to see how the whole process worked. As the court case proceeded, I just sat there and listened. As an intern, I was really only there to observe. The case was a family dispute and the judge came to a decision pretty quickly.

As I waited for him to swing the gavel and say, "Court dismissed," I heard the judge say something entirely unexpected. He looked over at me and said, "And what brings you here today young man?"

I stood to my feet. "Uhh, well, I'm an intern your honor," I managed to sputter.

"Do you plan to be a case worker when you graduate?" He asked. I started feeling uncomfortable. In a room full of people waiting for the court case to be dismissed, I wasn't sure why this judge was striking up a conversation with me.

"No sir, I don't," I replied.

He then asked me what I planned to do once I got my degree. At this point people throughout the courtroom were turning around in their seats and starring at me. "I'm going to go into ministry sir," I told him.

"And what type of ministry young man?" He asked.

"Well, music ministry." With that, I expected the conversation to be over. Already the awkwardness of the moment was obvious. In a courtroom full of people, I had no idea why this judge had singled me out. Then the judge did something even more unexpected.

"Music ministry," he said. "Do you sing?" I told him that I did. The judge smiled at me with a broad inviting smile and said, "Will you sing us a song?"

I couldn't believe what I was hearing. In the middle of a court case, this judge I've never seen before was asking me to sing a song. I froze. I told him I didn't have my guitar. He asked me to sing anyway.

So there I was, an intern in a courtroom full of people as the judge waited for me to sing. I quickly asked the Holy Spirit what I should sing, and then started in on a song I had just recently written. It explained the need for people to come to Christ and leave behind an empty life without God. After the song, the room was silent. We stood there for what felt like an eternity in the silence. The judge looked at my supervisor and asked her plainly, "Do you believe that Jesus is the only way to God?" She is a strong believer and didn't hesitate.

"Yes I do your honor," She replied. Then he asked me the same question. I told him I did. The judge leaned back in his seat.

"Thank you young man," he said. "You made my day." With that, the court was dismissed, and we all filed out of the courtroom. I couldn't believe what had just happened.

This experience is an illustration that of the final piece of the believers identity. It's true that we need to know that we're His children, and it's true that we need a revelation of His cleansing work in our hearts. We also need to experience the freedom from sin that Jesus makes available. But nothing in life is quite as fun as being His partner.

As we allow Him, the kingdom seeps into every area of life, and God allows us to partner with Him at the grocery store, the gas station, and at Christmas dinner with the family. He even lets us represent Him in the courtroom. Partnering with God means being His representative to an empty world. It means that you bring His kingdom or His rulership wherever you are. It goes beyond something you do, and becomes a part of who you are. You are an ambassador for the great God and this is the highest purpose life could ever have. It's not a life about you—it's about Him and you together. It's about a great God who chooses to love and to fellowship with us.

Identity is a powerful thing and finding the real you is a lifelong journey. Just because you know how you are doesn't mean you know who you are. If we want to bring a fresh model of what it means to follow Jesus, we have to spend some time here. You can't hide behind a flaky self image based on the grades you got in school, or your funny personality, or the money you make. We must be sons and daughters of our Father. We must be rooted and grounded in His love. Then, with His view of us, we can take on the world and watch the sparks fly.

Chapter 4
BECOMING INTENTIONAL

It was March 25th, 1739. The weather was clear and chilly that day at Hannam Mount in Kingswood, England. People had gathered by the thousands from all over the countryside. They came in carriages and on horseback, some of them traveling all night. Over twenty-three thousand people had gathered on this particular day. They stood in the vast field, waiting for the boy-preacher to appear. Finally, he came into view.

His appearance was nothing out of the ordinary. He was of average height and build, and he wore the formal gown of a minister. He carried no Bible and stood behind no pulpit. Instead, he stood on an old table and addressed the vast crowd. His voice was like the voice of a lion and it sang like a beautiful song. Those at the very edge of the crowd could distinguish every word. Before long, the power of his words began to change the atmosphere. All across the field, people started to weep under the power and the conviction of the Holy Spirit. First one, then another, then another.

On the morning of March 25th, 1739, as this young man in his early twenties explained the love of Christ, thousands repented of their sins and surrendered their hearts to God. I can only begin to imagine in my mind the awe and the wonder that must have filled Hannam Mount that day.

George Whitefield was a different kind of man. He was a kingdom man, and like John the Baptist before him, Whitefield had one foot in eternity for most of his life. As a young minister in England, his passion and fire for God caused many more reserved preachers to prohibit him from preaching in their churches. Whitefield didn't seem to mind. He turned to the open fields and began to preach. Soon news of his sermons spread like fire and thousands were coming to hear him. By the time he turned twenty-four, George Whitefield had preached to more people than any man who had ever lived. He crossed the Atlantic Ocean numerous times in his life and saw crowds of over fifty thousand gather in the American colonies to hear the gospel. God used him, along with a team of friends, to spark what historians call the Great Awakening, where nearly two-thirds of American colonists encountered God and were born-again.

Religious leaders of his day called Whitefield "extravagantly ridiculous," and in some ways, he was. He would often preach more than ten times a week and he would regularly ride on horseback through the night to reach his next location. He was a man of radical prayer and of radical vision, often spending the entire night in prayer. He asked God to use his life to set the world on fire, and God honored his request. It wasn't his talent, his education, or his social status that set George Whitefield apart. It was his single focus. He recorded the deepest cry of his heart in his journal as a young man. "God give me a deep humility, a well-guided zeal, a burning love, and a single eye, and then let men or devils do their worst." George Whitefield had eyes that saw the target.

I love to read about men like Whitefield. Something about his life lights a fire in my own heart. I'm challenged by the courage and passion that he operated in. One onlooker described him this way: "He looks almost angelic...a young, slim, slender youth before some thousands of people with a bold, undaunted countenance...For he looked as if he was clothed with authority from the great God." The truth is, if God would give that type of courage to men like Whitefield, Wesley,

Luther and countess others, why not to you and me for our generation?

In the past three chapters, we've discussed three different changes in our perspective. The first change has to do with the realization that we are in the midst of an emergency. The second perspective change deals with shifting our priorities in life and aligning our priorities with God's eternal perspective. The third change deals with discovering our true identity as followers of Jesus. All of these changes make up an entirely new way of seeing the world and inspire a new way of living. They challenge and provoke me to change, and I hope that they are making you a little uncomfortable with business as usual.

The last perspective change that's dealt with in this chapter is the catalyst for the rest of the book. It's the truth that propels us to live the practices outlined in Part 2. Simply put, the perspective change is to move from passivity to intentionality. It's when we stop waiting for God to move and we start moving.

Imagine for a minute that you had a chance to go back to Biblical times and had arranged to go on a fishing trip with the Apostle Peter. He meets you at the dock by his boat and within a few minutes, you're on the open sea. After sailing for a while, you finally reach an ideal spot and Peter puts in the anchor and sits down on the bench, smiling with anticipation. You're excited too. You can't wait to spend time with the great apostle and learn a little bit about fishing, too. Minutes go by, and you start to wonder why you are both idly sitting there. "Well, what's next?" You ask. He just sits there smiling at you. "Do we use fishing poles?" He shakes his head no. "Of course not," You say, "We use nets." Now he's grinning from ear to ear.

"Not today," he replies.

"Do we use any sort of bait?"

"No bait."

Now you're completely confused. You are no expert fisherman, but this doesn't make any sense. Finally, you decide to just ask the obvious question, "How do we catch the fish, Peter?" The great apostle leans in close to you, as if he's about to disclose an important secret. His sun-scorched forehead is nearly touching yours.

Finally, he whispers, "Today, I wanted to try out a strategy that I've seen the church in your generation use when catching men. We are going to sit here, in this ideal location, and wait for the fish to jump in the boat! I'm sure that some of the fish will be attracted to this beautiful vessel and just jump right on the deck!"

After a few hours in the scorching sun, Peter would have successfully made his point. The most effective way to catch fish is to go where they are, and not wait for them to come to where you are. When George Whitefield wanted to reach the world, he didn't go to the church; he went to the fields—and soon the churches were filled. When Peter wanted to catch fish, he put his nets in the sea, and soon the deck of his ship was overflowing with fish.

We've got to get a glimpse of how the kingdom works. Jesus tries to explain it to us in Matthew 11:12. He tells us that "the kingdom of heaven suffers violence, and violent men take it by force." The passage isn't endorsing a physically violent revolution. The word "violent" is also translated "forceful" or "energetic". The point that He is trying to make is that the things of God won't fall into your lap. They must be pursued, sought after, and sometimes wrestled to the ground until all the fullness of God is real in your life. We don't earn the things of God—we never could. But we fight for them and the fight is a fight to believe in a world we can't see. We must develop a violent and intentional determination to pull the kingdom of heaven down to earth.

Somehow, in our generation, we have adopted a passive and unintentional approach to life and to God. We think that people will be reached with God's love if we open the doors of the church. We think that the scripture will transform our minds if we casually read it for a few minutes every morning. We think that God will hear our prayers and answer them if we take a couple of seconds while we're driving to work to say hello and make our requests. This is not the way it works. If we want to find the things that God offers His children and if we want to make an eternal impact in this world, then we must be strategic. We must become intentional.

THE STRATEGIC PLAN

In the book of Romans, the Apostle Paul outlines God's divine strategy for reaching the world with His love. It's the only strategy outlined in scripture to reach the world. God doesn't outline a plan B or plan C anywhere. The plan has six steps, and its pretty simple. They are: sent—preach—hear—believe—call—saved (Romans 10:13-15). It begins with being sent. This means that followers of Jesus must leave their comfortable surroundings and go places where they will find people who need Jesus. We are God's strategy to introduce the world to the kingdom. The "sent" part of the strategy is not just for missionaries and traveling preachers. It's for every single follower of Jesus. This could mean that you're sent to your friend's cubicle at work, or some kid's locker at school or the Denny's across the street. To reach people and make a difference, we first must go.

After believers are sent, we then preach to those who don't know God. As people hear the truth, some will believe, call on God, and be saved. In this way, God intends to reach the world with the gospel. This may seem overly simplified to you, but this basic strategy generates powerful results. The only trick is it doesn't work if you remove one of the links in the chain.

For most of us, the problem begins with step one. We never go. We never intentionally walk out of our front door in the morning thinking, "I am leaving my home today to win the world to Jesus. I am going to be

His representative to this lost world." Instead, we're focused on hundreds of other things that we must accomplish during our day. Often, we intentionally plan time to go shopping, go to the movies, or get our haircut, but we don't plan time to reach people. This is completely backwards.

Being sent might mean moving to Africa or Asia as a missionary for the gospel. It might mean talking to your friend over a cheeseburger, visiting the elderly in a nursing home, or praying for the sick at a hospital. Africa is no more spiritual than your desk at school. Regardless of where you are, the idea is to use your day to bring God's kingdom into every situation.

Once we are sent, it doesn't stop there. Next, we preach. Preaching doesn't mean that we stand behind a pulpit in an expensive suit and gather "amen's" from a crowd. That's not the essence of preaching. To preach means to proclaim with our lifestyle and with our words the freedom of redemption in Jesus. It has nothing to do with the tone of your voice or the college degree you hold. It has everything to do with spreading truth.

If we are faithful to go and preach, something magical will happen. It's like pushing a huge green button in Heaven that starts a series of supernatural events. Without any effort, those who "go" and "preach" will stand in awe as God takes over and His power is released. People will hear, believe, call and be saved and we have the honor of rejoicing with them.

For a long time, I didn't believe that it was that easy to unlock God's power--until I met Marge. Marge lives with her husband and their two kids a few towns over from me. She is a social worker and attended the church that I went to as a teenager. I first met Marge years ago at my youth group and as soon as we met, I noticed something distinguishably different about her. I picked up on it right away. When she walks in the room there's something that draws people to her. If Marge walked into your house today, she'd probably be wearing a sweatshirt and a pair of jeans with sneakers and she would have a pleasant smile on her face as she approached you. Her casual style and demeanor make people comfortable around her right away. But it is not these things that really set Marge apart. There's something else.

Spend a day with her and you would pick up on it too. She files papers, visits clients for her work, meets with supervisors, but through all her tasks and responsibilities, her focus never changes. Like no one I've ever met, Marge has a gift to intentionally, tactfully introduce Jesus wherever she goes. In fact, years ago Marge shared with me a bold prayer that she prayed. She told Jesus, "Lord, every day I'm alive I'll look for opportunities to share the gospel and I'll step out and take the opportunities that You bring me. Allow me to lead someone to You *every day*, God."

When she first told me about her prayer, I thought she was crazy. Every day! Is that even possible?

In the first chapter of this book I mentioned that the average Christian dies without leading a single person to faith in Christ. If this is true, how could one person lead someone to Jesus every day?

I remember one experience with Marge walking out of her office after she had a long day of difficult work. She was sharing with me some of the current concerns she had with a client. Then, as we turned the corner, Marge's spiritual awareness kicked in. She noticed a lady who looked troubled standing alone on the steps. Marge engaged the woman in a conversation and within ten minutes the woman was crying as she prayed with Marge to get right with God. If I asked Marge about that day, she probably wouldn't remember it. It's not that she doesn't care, or that it wasn't important to her. It's just that she had three hundred and sixty four other encounters like this one during the course of that year. She led at least one person to Christ every day for three years. For her, it wasn't an impossible prayer. It's her lifestyle.

Marge has a gift. She may be the most effective witness for Jesus I know. Just being around her challenges me to share my faith. Recently, I decided to make an effort to share the gospel with at least one person every day for a week. To be completely honest, I allowed my schedule and responsibilities to get in the way and I missed a couple of days. The experience made me even more amazed at the way that God uses Marge day after day, week after week, but I don't believe that

that kind of effectiveness is reserved only for a select few.

I'm not saying that God wants us to live under some legalistic condemnation where we feel like we constantly need to "hit our numbers." We don't earn brownie points with God when we share our faith. Remember, the child of God is blameless through Jesus. We do however, participate in the most important work on planet earth and this work must be taken seriously.

What makes Marge so effective as a witness for Christ? Without a doubt, her effectiveness comes from her ability to maintain her focus. She almost never preaches behind a pulpit. She doesn't lead a world-renowned, million-dollar ministry. She works for a secular, state run, social service agency. Her secret isn't in her title or her occupation. Marge focuses on two simple truths: First, that she is sent to reach the people around her for Christ, and second that she will share the love of God with others as God provides the opportunities. As these first two parts of Romans 10 are followed, the other four fall into place.

I will be the first to admit that sharing about Jesus in some situations can be uncomfortable. I've also seen people preach Jesus because they feel guilty if they don't and they never come off right. The chief strategy of the kingdom is love and love must be at the heart of every effort. At the same time, we don't have to add anything to the truth. It may feel awkward, but the gospel of the kingdom carries a power of its own to save and restore those who will respond. It is the power of God for salvation (Rom 1:16).

Unfortunately, this truth is often the last thing that believers share with unbelievers. We'll talk about our church and its programs. We'll talk about our Christian music or our Christian activities, but we often neglect to share the very truth that has the power of God to change a life. It's not enough to just be nice to people. It's not enough to listen to Christian music or wear a Christian tee-shirt. We must share the good news that God came to earth, died for our sins, rose again, and made all things new and when we do, the power of God will follow.

DIVINE RESPONSIBILITY

What motivated George Whitefield to risk his life and cross the dangerous waters of the Atlantic Ocean time after time to reach the American colonies with the gospel? What made him ride on horseback through the night, just to preach the next day? What motives Marge to carve out time day after day to share with people? For them, it's not because a preacher told them to witness. It's gone deeper in their hearts than that. They must share God's love. They feel personally responsible to reach the lost.

In Ezekiel, chapter 33, God outlines what He required of Ezekiel. He explains that Ezekiel was the spiritual watchman for the people of Israel, and just as a watchman stands on the wall and keeps watch for any approaching danger, so God required Ezekiel to keep watch over Israel's spiritual condition. God goes on to explain that if He tells Ezekiel to warn the wicked about the penalty for their sins, and Ezekiel does not do it, the wicked will die for their sins, but their blood will be required of Ezekiel. If he wasn't faithful to warn the wicked, their blood would be on his hands (Ezekiel 33:2-9).

In the New Testament, Jesus explains that believers are the light of the world. God has given us the divine responsibility to be watchmen for our generation and this means that we are responsible, just as Ezekiel was, to warn the wicked of their sins. We carry that mandate. How could we possibly stand back and take it lightly? How can we casually live life without passion and purpose while our friends, and family members, and neighbors, stumble around in darkness?

When this divine responsibility starts to seep past your head and gets into your heart, it will make you do some crazy things. You'll start developing a plan to reach your friends and family members for Jesus. You'll start looking at every situation from a new perspective. This divine responsibility will be the catalyst to push you toward a new place and following Jesus becomes more and more an adventure and less a responsibility.

FINDING GOD

It's true that we must become intentional about reaching the lost, but becoming intentional isn't just about reaching the world. This principle of intentionality has application in every area of the believer's life. Remember Jesus said that the kingdom suffers violence. That means every aspect of God's kingdom.

One way that I have found helps me develop this principle in my life is to find it at work in other people. Marge showed me what it looks like to be an intentional witness for Christ. It was my friend Nick who taught me intentional spiritual growth.

Nick is a pretty average guy—at first glance. He's a gym teacher in Wilmington, Delaware, and teaches elementary school kids about physical fitness and sports. In actuality, the school is in such a rough section of town that Nick's main focus is to keep his kids so worn out and busy with their exercises that they don't have any energy left to kill each other. Almost every kid in his gym class comes from a fatherless home. Most of them are surrounded by drugs and violence every day. Nick grew up in white suburbia, but the voice of God led him to downtown Wilmington.

I first met Nick when I was a teenager. He is a few years older than I am, and we became friends at a Christian camp where he was a counselor and I was a camper. If Nick walked in to the room where you're reading this, he'd probably be wearing gym shorts and a tee-shirt. You would notice his wide smile that stretches from one end of his face to the other. He wouldn't force his way into a conversation with you. That's not really his style. But if you were lucky enough to talk with him for a few minutes, or a few hours, you would inevitably realize the incredible depth of spiritual insight that he has. If you were looking with your new eyes, you would become aware of the fact that Nick walks with God.

From the first time we met, I realized that I could learn a lot from Nick's personal walk with God. He was intentional about his growth as a follower of Jesus. He deeply studied scripture and had a broad understanding of the Word. He spent long hours in prayer, learning to hear God's voice. I wanted that kind of spiritual life and I wanted to know God like he did.

One day, I decided to ask him how he had developed such a close relationship with the Holy Spirit. His response was classic. I was looking for some deep theological explanation, but instead Nick just taught me about becoming intentional. He looked at me, leaned back, and put his hands behind his head. Then he gave me one of those broad smiles. "It's simple," he said. "You've gotta want it."

Spiritual growth doesn't just happen. People don't get close to God because of their personality, or because they got lucky. People get close to God because they intentionally pursue Him, just like people come to salvation when Christians intentionally share their faith. The responsibility to grow is on us. It's true that God actually causes the growth, but we have got to do the things necessary to make growth possible. Just like the farmer who plants and waters, we must be intentional about a spiritual harvest. The earth causes the seed to grow, not the farmer, but the seed would never have a chance if the farmer hadn't planted it and watered it every day. My spiritual growth depends on my daily, intentional pursuit of God.

I said at the beginning of this chapter that the new perspective introduced here was to move from passivity to intentionality. The reason I said that, is because I think that this is a big problem that demands a change in perspective. If the responsibility to reach others is on me, what happens if I do nothing? If the responsibility for others to grow closer to God is on me, what happens if I don't invest in that relationship? The reality of our responsibility is both heavy and freeing. It's heavy because it means that we have to start doing something. It's freeing because it means that our actions have the power to change our direction and will make a world of difference.

THE PRACTICE

As God began to unfold this idea of becoming intentional in my life, I decided right away to put it into practice. The problem I ran into was figuring out the balance. I decided I would regularly share my faith, study the scripture, pray and serve those in need. I would fellowship with other believers, worship, teach and help the poor. I tried to balance all the different aspects of the Christian life, but I always felt like I was not doing enough of something. I would witness, but neglect my prayer time. I would study scripture, but not help the poor. I found myself always feeling like I wasn't doing enough for God. Maybe you've tried this and struggled with the same feelings. Then God began to show me a secret.

In the gospel of John, Jesus talks about this idea of new eyes. He tells us that, "The Son can do nothing of Himself, unless it is something *He sees* the Father doing" (John 8:19 emphasis added). Jesus is teaching us that an intentional mindset must work in unity with spiritual awareness. Jesus came to die on the cross for the sins of the world—He was focused on His assignment—but He was also sensitive to the Father's leading and direction. It's not enough to create a long list of your goals as a follower of God. Those goals must be submitted to the daily leading of God's Holy Spirit. Becoming intentional means deeply knowing the values of eternity and purposefully acting on those values, but it's not robotic. It's fluid. It's not about meeting a quota. It's about moment by moment being aware of God and what He wants you to do.

Marge wakes up every morning focused on leading someone to Christ, but her focus is partnered with spiritual sensitivity to the opportunities and leading of God. I've talked to her since that three year period of leading someone to Jesus every day and that season came to an end. She's not condemned about it, and she is still an incredibility affective witness. Nick sets time aside daily to develop his prayer life and his knowledge of scripture, but if the Holy Spirit directs him to pray as he sits down to read, Nick changes direction. More than anything, becoming intentional means intentionally developing your pursuit of God and your awareness of God's leading. You can't ever pray enough, and you can't ever witness enough, but this isn't an excuse to be passive. We've already discussed that if we are going to advance God's kingdom, we must do it with spiritual "violence" or forcefulness.

It's been said that the person who aims at nothing, hits it every time. We will never make an impact for God until we bury this passive, inactive approach to life and develop a lifestyle that reaches the heart of God and the needs of the world. Like George Whitefield, those who live for another world have a single eye.

I recently heard a story about two young men who felt called by God to be missionaries. For weeks, they prayed and asked God where they should go. Finally, these young men decided that God was calling them to this one particular remote village deep in the heart of Africa. As the boys researched this village, and the tribe that occupied the area, they learned that this tribe had never heard the gospel of Jesus Christ before. They also learned that this tribe was completely opposed to outsiders being allowed into their village. Any outsider that came in and tried to live among them would be killed. The only way to enter the village as an outsider was to enter as a slave.

Selling themselves as slaves was not what these young men had imagined when they thought of missions work. If they did this, it would be for life. They would probably be treated poorly by their master, and they would never see their friends and families again. They knew that making this decision would cost them everything.

As they wrestled with the decision, they could not escape the fact that God was calling them to bring His kingdom to this tribe.   Their hearts broke for the tribesmen as they realized that the village had no hope of eternal life outside of Christ. If God had truly called them, and they didn't go, the blood of these people was on their hands.

Finally, these two young men made their decision. They would sell themselves as slaves and give their lives to reach this tribe with the gospel of Christ. As they boarded the ship for Africa, their friends and family members came to the dock to say their final goodbyes. Realizing that she would never see her son again, one of the boys mother ran to the end of the dock as the boat began to move out of the harbor. Her son rushed to the edge of the ship, and their eyes met. From the deck of the ship, he raised his hand in the air and shouted across the harbor, "To win for the Lamb the rewards of His suffering." This was the last time anyone saw those two boys. They spent the rest of their lives buried deep in the heart of an African village bringing eternal hope to a group of people who had no other chance of redemption.

Focus makes all the difference in the world. The type of radical commitment displayed by these two heroes intimidates the bravest among us, but within every believer, there is the capacity to be a spiritual giant. It begins with new eyes. These two young men saw the need, felt the call, and couldn't escape it. The next step is to get on the boat. They allowed their new perspective to completely alter their lifestyle. They found the new road and it took them to their calling. Maybe like never before, you are starting to see that God is calling you to a higher place. It's time to walk down that new road and discover the adventure that He has prepared for you.

Part 2
A New Road
PRACTICES OF AN AWAKENED LIFE

You may have heard the story of the man and the ditch. The man left his house one day and walked to work. On his way, he fell in to a ditch that was in the middle to the road. The ditch was deep and the man was bruised and dirty from his fall.

The next day, before the man left his house he prayed that God would keep him from falling in the ditch again. He walked down the same road to work, and on his way he found himself stumbling into the same ditch. The man was bruised and dirty again.

On the third day, the man was very careful and walked very cautiously to work. He noticed the ditch just before his foot reached it, and he fell only half-way in to the ditch.

On the fourth day, the man was thoroughly prepared. He had drawn up a map of just where the ditch was and set an alarm on his cell phone to beep just before he arrived at the location of the ditch. The road however, was full of traffic and noise, and there was construction that day and the man could barely hear the beeping of his alarm. He did manage to only slightly stumble over the ditch.

On the fifth day, the man walked down a different road. He never fell in the ditch again.

Sometimes, we need to find a new road. Life won't change until we begin to develop new practices based on our new beliefs. It's not enough to have good ideas. We've got to be able to live them if we want to see anything change. The second half of this book will discuss some practices of an awakened life.

Chapter 5
THE GARDEN

I gave my life to Jesus as a teenager at a full gospel inner-city church in New Haven, Connecticut. It was everything a good old-fashioned born-again experience should be. I cried, I went forward, and I prayed the prayer with the pastor. Then I did it again the next week, and the week after that, and the week after that. Finally, someone explained to me that I didn't need to get "re-saved" every time I sinned. They told me that I needed to start what they called a "daily walk" with God, so I started putting time aside every day and waiting for

God to show up. This was the humble start of my journey to find the secret place.

The first Christian songs I ever heard were, *Look What the Lord has Done*, and *Ancient of Days*. It wasn't until I was in college that I encountered a hymnal. While most young people may be tired of hymnals, I was fascinated by them. These collections of ancient songs rich with meaning captured my creativity and intrigued me. Finally, I asked a friend of mine who attended a Baptist Church to see if I could borrow one of the churches hymnals. He produced the book, and I never asked any questions.

It was then that I stumbled upon the hymn, *In the Garden*. Here are the words, straight out of the same hymnal that I'm still borrowing from my friend's church:

> "I come to the garden alone, while the dew is still on the roses; and the voice I hear, falling on my ear, the Son of God discloses.
> He speaks, and the sound of His voice is so sweet the birds hush their singing; and the melody that He gave to me, within my heart is ringing.
> And He walks with me and He talks with me, and He tells me I am His own, and the joy we share as we tarry there, none other has ever known.
> I would stay in the garden with Him though the night around me be falling; But He bids

me to go through the voice of woe, His voice
to me is calling."

I recently preached at a church service and at the end of the meeting, one of the elders of the church called me in to the office and asked me for some personal prayer. He looked at me with tears streaming down his cheeks. "Honestly," he said, "I've been a Christian for over 20 years and I am still not sure that I have a real relationship with God. I read the Bible and pray just about every day, but I think I've felt His presence maybe twice in my entire life." He looked in to my eyes and I could sense his desperation. "I want more than that," he told me.

This church elder is not unique. Maybe you're in exactly the same place. We hear a lot about a personal relationship with God in Christian circles today, but what does that really look like? Is it all about discipline and daily devotions, or is it all about feeling something? Can we actually know God and cultivate a real personal relationship with Him? As followers of Jesus, what does a personal walk with God look like?

If you read the words of Jesus in the New Testament, you definitely get the sense that He knew the Father really well. Jesus talked about God like He was His best friend, and He loved the Father in an intimate way. He told His followers that we should go to the Father "who is in secret." This implies that there's a secret place where it's only you and God; a place that only the two of you share.

Is there really a garden where you can meet with God and walk with Him and hear His voice? And if there is, how do you get there? And even if you can get there, is that essential to being a successful follower of Jesus?

There is a garden. There is a place of real living, breathing intimacy with God in this lifetime. We don't have to wait for Heaven to hear God and know God. There's a way to get to the garden, and being in that place is like water to your spirit. Maybe you've been there—you know. I've been there and I want to live in God's tangible presence every moment of every day. God desires to show His children the path that leads to this place. Let's explore together.

ACTIVITY VERSES PRODUCTIVITY

In the spring of 2004 I entered in to one of the craziest times of my life. I didn't know it then, but God would use this season to teach me a powerful lesson. In the course of six weeks, I bought a house, got married, wrote a 100-page thesis, graduated college, moved out of my apartment, and birthed a full-time traveling ministry. The stress and the chaos of that time was intense. Between wedding preparations and fund-raising, I needed to find time to write college papers and learn about real estate. I remember the night where I couldn't handle it anymore. I collapsed in exhaustion at the foot of my bed and called out to God. "Father, this is ridiculous. I can't do all this. How do you expect me to handle all this at once? How do I do it?"

I had reached my limit. I couldn't push anymore. It was at that moment that the quiet voice of the Holy Spirit broke through my fatigue and spoke to my soul. He whispered very clearly, *"Double your time in prayer."* As soon as I heard those words, a cold chill ran down my spine. It's the feeling I sometimes get when I know God has said something, but it runs contrary to everything my natural mind wants to hear. I just sat there stunned for a few seconds.

The only word I could manage was, "What?"

Again He spoke, *"Double your time in prayer."* Right away my thoughts started to shoot around the room and bounce off the walls as my mind wrestled with the idea. I had already committed an hour every day to prayer and Bible study for my personal time with God. The idea of two hours a day seemed like the perfect way to go insane. How could I even consider making a commitment like that while I was barely getting in my hour? As I knelt there on the floor in my apartment, the idea swirled around me. Something deep inside knew that God was speaking to me and the idea to double my time couldn't possibly have been something from my own mind.

I had reached one of those crazy trust moments where God was asking me to completely ignore my rational mind and believe His voice. I had a sense that He was trying to teach me something big—something that would impact all of my decisions in the future.

I sat there and smiled. It just seemed laughable. "Okay, God," I said. "Let's do it—two hours a day."

That was my first step down a new road. I realized that God's way of getting things done runs completely contrary to our way of getting things done. God was teaching me the solution to my overworking. Activity does not produce spiritual fruitfulness. *Intimacy and only intimacy produces fruitfulness.*

Think about the implications of this truth. The life of Jesus is a perfect example of intimacy producing fruitfulness. He spent the first thirty years of His earthly life in the poor section of Israel called Nazareth. He was unknown to the world. Imagine being the Son of God, and living incognito for your first thirty years! Most of us wouldn't make it thirty minutes before we would start showcasing our gifts to the world! He worked as a carpenter, and then at age thirty began His ministry. It lasted only three years and he never once left His tiny country. He never held any public office and He barely had national attention, yet somehow His short life on earth made Him the most influential person in all of human history.

Jesus completely changed the course of the human race, but He didn't do it through fame, money, influence, or power—His strategy was completely different. The plan was simply to do only what He saw His Father in Heaven doing. He walked in perfect intimacy with the Father and that produced the most fruitful life that ever lived.

As a follower of Jesus, I can spend my whole life trying in my power and through my planning to do something big for His kingdom. The problem is that God didn't design human beings to function this way. We aren't supposed to produce fuel internally. Instead, we are supposed to fuel up through our relationship with God. Just as a gasoline car can't go anywhere without gasoline, it's equally true that *apart from Him, I can do nothing* (John 15:5). Think about that—nothing.

Only a life that is deeply connected to God in an intimate, personal way will actually make an eternal impact. In order to become fruitful for God, we have to fully surrender the idea that we can accomplish eternal things in our own strength. Eternal priorities can only be accomplished by those who have come to the end of their own efforts and are whole-heartedly dedicated to intimacy with Jesus above all else.

So, that day in 2004 I made a commitment to God to spend two hours alone with Him in prayer. At first, it was pretty tough. I was still really stressed about all of life's chaos and none of it disappeared. Then, slowly, I began to reach new levels of intimacy in my time with God. He revealed to me the secret found in 1 Peter 5. Peter told us to, "Humble ourselves under the mighty hand of God...casting all your anxiety on Him, because He cares for you" (1 Peter 5:6-7). God showed me that to hold on to my fears and anxieties is a form of spiritual pride. By being anxious I am telling God that He's not big enough to carry my problems so I'll carry them for Him. Anxiety about problems is proof that I'm not fully giving those problems to my Father.

There's a good side too. Peter tells us that God gives grace to those who are humble. James calls it "the greater grace" (James 4:6). Grace can be defined as unmerited favor—power beyond my own ability. This means that if I humble myself and fully trust the outcome of all things to God, He will release His greater grace. As soon as we do this, God releases a power beyond our own ability that makes impossible things possible. So God's strategy is this: Believe Him for all He has promised, humble yourself and cast your anxiety on Him and your faith will release a greater grace that allows the impossible to materialize!

I began casting all my concerns on God and soon, crazy things started to happen. It was like a switch was turned on in Heaven, and a fresh divine favor started following me around. I'll never forget the day that I walked in to the Dean's office at my university. I needed him to sign an approval for my thesis. I was expected to have a thorough outline of what my thesis was about and how I would do the research. I handed the Dean the packet to sign, but it was completely blank. I had been spending two hours with God, writing other college papers, working with lawyers to buy a house, and fund raising for ministry and I hadn't had time to outline the thesis.

The Dean looked at me, smiled and said, "It looks like everything is on course." At first, I thought he was kidding. Then I stood there, with my jaw hanging around my kneecaps in disbelief as he signed his signature of approval and handed me back the packet! He had never opened it to realize that the packet had no content! (Don't get me wrong—I'm not saying you can get out of work. I still worked hard on my thesis and got a high score).

Later that month, I put an offer in on a house. The problem was that we had no down payment. We had sought God, and felt like we should make the offer anyways. We decided to put in an incredibly low offer, so I never expected the owner to actually accept it. Twenty-four hours later, I got a phone call that the offer was accepted and I needed $10,000 the next day! Of course, we had no money. A family member contacted us and told us that they would loan us the money. When we met them to pick up the check, they let us know that the $10,000 wasn't a loan—it was a gift!

In the following months, we watched as God provided an additional $10,000 to pay the rest of the down payment. As a twenty-one year old college student, I didn't even have a real job! We stood back in awe as we realized what Jesus meant when He said, "Seek first His kingdom and His righteousness and all these things will be added to you" (Matthew 6:33). It's not about getting out of writing college papers, or getting God to give you money. It's about trusting God in all things and putting your intimacy with Him above everything else in life, and then trusting Him for provision and favor through all of life's challenges. This doesn't mean that following God is palm trees and sunshine and everything is happy and wonderful all the time. It does mean that when we focus our internal eyes on Him, the Holy Spirit will guide us on His perfect path. Intimacy produces fruitfulness.

Years ago, I read the story of Richard Wurmbrand, the founder of Voice of the Martyrs. He spent over ten years in communist prison being tortured because of his unwavering dedication to Jesus. He was drugged, beaten, and abused for days and months and years on end. In reflecting back on those years of prison, Wurmbrand has often called them glorious. But how could they be? That probably wouldn't be one of the first words I would use to explain an experience like his.

I once heard a sermon by Wurmbrand and he told the story about the day he was released from his cell and told that he could go home. As he walked outside and the gate to the compound closed behind him, he looked up to God and said, "Father I thank you, not so much that I have been released from prison, but more so that while I have been in prison you have been with me every moment." Richard Wurmbrand knew the secret. Intimacy produces fruitfulness.

THE ONE THING

Have you ever burned out spiritually? Have you ever been lit on fire for God at a conference or a church service and then seen that fire slowly die until you could hardly remember what it was like? Did you know that God has provided a way for us to avoid spiritual burnout?

I burned out once in my life. By God's grace I hope to never burn out again. For me, it was three years into full-time ministry and God had opened numerous doors for us. I allowed myself to become so busy with ministry that my intimate time with God became preparation time for the next event. One day I realized that I loved ministry, but my love for Him had grown cold. It took me two months to break the funk.

It's not enough to have time with Him every day. The focus of my love and my affection must be for Him— not for my vision, my future, or what He can give me. Simply being with Jesus must be my one great passion; my one thing. Now, almost every day I ask myself, "Do I love the Father, Son and Holy Spirit more than I love the vision?" It's a way to refocus and not run out of fuel.

I believe that King David in the Bible uncovered this truth. He wrote in Psalm 27:4, *"One thing I have asked from the Lord, that I shall seek; that I may dwell in the house of the Lord all the days of my life, to behold the beauty of the Lord and to meditate in His temple."* Notice that David didn't say that his "one thing" was to be blessed by God or to have God answer his requests. Instead, David's one thing was to be close to God.

Mary, the sister of Lazarus and Martha, also found the one thing. She discovered the garden where the lover of God will never run dry. When Jesus came to visit Mary's family, her sister Martha ran around like a maniac, trying to prepare the house for their guest. Mary just sat at the feet of Jesus. Jesus told Martha, "You are worried and bothered about so many things; but only *one thing* is necessary, for Mary has chosen the good part, which shall not be taken away from her" (Luke 10:41-42 emphasis added).

I think so often, we run around with preparations for Christian stuff and our love and affection for Jesus dries up. Christianity becomes a program and a system, and God is left waiting outside. Discovering the "one thing" means unlocking real fruitfulness by keeping intimacy with God our life's priority.

The Apostle Paul found the one thing. The Amplified Bible tells us that Paul's great passion was to "progressively become more deeply and intimately acquainted with Him" (Phil 3:10). David, Mary, and Paul each cultivated within their souls a desperate desire to know God. Knowing Him and loving Him became their great passion—they focused their entire lives around intimacy with Jesus. Just like my experience with doubling my time in prayer, something electric and supernatural happens when we focus on knowing God as our great priority.

THE POWER OF FOCUS

I remember as a young kid the day I got my first magnifying glass. I was probably eight years old and my mom gave it to me as part of a kid's detective kit. I looked through the glass and realized that it made things look bigger. It wasn't doing a whole lot for me at first.

It wasn't until my best friend "Wild Will" came over that my young mind grasped the full potential of this lethal weapon. Will took me outside, started flipping over some rocks, and quickly collected a few slugs and worms. He then angled the magnifying glass so that it caught the sunlight and channeled its power. I watched in awe and delight as the slug made a slight hissing sound and then exploded in a fury of electric fire! Soon, we were optimizing the potential of my new toy to harness the sunlight and roast leaves, ants, and anything else we could find.

Focus generates power. If you focus your life on intimacy with God above all else, the power then becomes available for all other areas of life. To find the garden you need to make your growth towards God your focus.

Recently, I was a guest speaker at a youth camp and I did a message on daily time with God. I gave the students an opportunity to ask questions, and one young man raised his hand and said, "I've tried to spend daily time with God before and it seems to get pushed out of a busy day. How do I avoid that?"

I answered, "It's simple, but it's not easy. Make your time with God more important than eating or sleeping. If you miss a meal or an hour of sleep, then so be it. If you take it that seriously, you'll almost never miss your time with God." I'm not sure how much the young man appreciated my answer, but it's still true. In a kingdom that advances by force, we've got to fight to find the garden.

One of my favorite passages in the entire Bible is Psalm 73:25. The psalmist wrote, "Whom have I in heaven but You? And besides You I desire nothing on earth." What an incredible statement. Nothing! Not a good job, a family, a lot of friends, a nice car, a big ministry—his devotion to God was so great that every other desire was like nothing compared to that one thing. Imagine what the world would look life if every Christian followed the simple truth that intimacy with Jesus and only intimacy produces fruitfulness.

MAKING IT REAL

Finding the garden and developing a lifestyle of knowing God is a process. It grows day by day. I want to share with you some things that have helped me in my journey. These aren't engraved on stone tablets— they're just some practical ideas to get you closer. Also, understand that I'm not advocating having time alone with Jesus and then shutting off the Jesus button and going about your day. Nothing could be further from the truth. Daily alone time with God is important because it enhances your ability to walk in fellowship during the times in life when the room is not quiet and you can't be alone. Hopefully, these practical things will spur you on.

To start, I've found that if I'm going to spend alone time with God, the location is extremely important. I want to be alone. Jesus told us, "When you pray, go into your most private room, and closing the door, pray to your Father..." (Matt 6:6 Amplified Bible). There's something about being totally alone that is instrumental in quieting your soul. No cell phone, no distractions. It's difficult enough to focus in our nanosecond society, so finding a quiet place is an absolute must. As a teenager, I could close the door in my bedroom and be alone. Once I went to college, I had to get a little more creative. I went everywhere from basements, to bathrooms, to stairwells just to find a secret place where no one could see me or hear me. Looking back, there were some awkward moments when another student occasionally would walk in during my prayer time to use the men's room in the basement of my dormitory!

Today, as part of a traveling ministry, finding quiet places is still a challenge. I've spent time alone with God in hotel hallways, the front seat of parked cars, out behind buildings, and in bathrooms more times than I can count. It's worth it. Being alone with Jesus is that important. I know that sometimes it's totally impossible to actually be physically alone. In those moments, I trust that God understands and that He'll still meet with me— and He does.

The time of day also makes a difference. Typically, I try to spend time alone with God the first thing in the morning, and the last thing at night. What's important is to find a time where you can give your undivided attention—not while driving a car (although you can pray then too!). You may already have a routine that works for you when it comes to daily time with God. I challenge you to try some of the ideas in this chapter and see if they take you deeper.

I want to break down the seven different areas of time with God that I practice. Hopefully, these will help you as you seek the secret place with God. I encourage you to use these as guideposts—don't go through some ritual. Instead, allow each of these areas to become real to you personally.

1. Worship

To worship God means to place Him in my heart where He belongs—at the top. It means that I tell Him and express to Him how incredible He is, not because He needs to hear it, but because I need to humble myself and admit His greatness and glory. Worshiping God puts me in the right position to interact with Him. Worship humbles my proud heart which allows me to hear His voice.

Imagine for a minute having a personal meeting with the President of the United States or the Queen of England. You would probably show them a considerable amount of honor—at least you should. How much more honor should we show the designer of creation! Nearly every time I am alone with God, I worship. It allows me to find proper perspective. He's God, and I'm not.

I find that praying in tongues has become a powerful part of my personal worship time. The Apostle Paul taught that he prayed and sang in his spiritual language (1 Corinthians 14:15). The Bible teaches that this spiritual language builds up the inner man, even though your mind doesn't know what you are saying. If you want to develop this gift in your life, pursue it. Ask God for it, and talk with those who operate in it (1 Corinthians 14). It will take you to a new, greater depth of worship.

I also love to sing to God. Sometimes I sing a well-known Christian song, and other times I just make up a song from my heart. Either way, God doesn't care how pretty we sound. A song from an honest heart is great music to Him.

Worship will open the door to the presence of God and as you learn to worship Him, you will learn what His presence feels like. It's not just an emotion. It's a spiritual sense of God's closeness. Some have described it as a warm blanket, or an inner peace. I don't know how to describe it other than a sense that God is near.

Sometimes in my alone time with God, His presence shows up immediately and other times I don't feel Him at all. I find that the more sensitive I am to His inner leading, the stronger and more consistent His presence becomes in my life. Don't be fooled—God is not a system, He's a person. For whatever reason, sometimes He will feel closer than other times. I believe that there are times where He will pull back the experience of His presence to push me to hunger after Him more. It's not science or arithmetic. It's relationship, and because of that, it can be messy and a bit unpredictable.

2. Meditating

The second piece of my time with God is meditation. I choose a few key scriptures that have to do with something I am trying to grow in, and I focus my full attention on the truth they contain. Sometimes, if I strongly sense the closeness of God, I've found that I don't need to say or do anything. There are times where He seems so close and all I want to do is stay right where I am. Hours have passed where I've said and done nothing. I've heard this experience being referred to as "beholding the Lord." Honestly, I'm not big on naming things, but I do know that while I'm there in His presence I can sense Him working within me, and transforming me from within (2 Corinthians 3:18). I've found that the more time I spend "beholding" the more spiritually sensitive I become to His inner voice.

In the beginning of my walk with God, meditating was really difficult because my mind wouldn't quiet down. It would run from one thought to the next and I wasn't able to focus. If that's your experience, there's hope! The more time you spend learning to focus, the easier it becomes. Keep setting aside time to focus your mind and quiet your soul. There will be times where you end up totally distracted, but don't let that discourage you. I think God is pleased with our effort and pursuit, and soon you'll start to hear His voice.

Maybe you've never felt God's presence before. I encourage you to get alone and begin to worship Him. I've found that faith is the key to getting closer to God. I've got to believe that He is willing and ready to meet with me. I've got to expect to find Him. If this is a struggle for you, go back to chapter 3 and mediate on the way God sees you. Renew your thinking.

This is where the Bible is so important. It tells us that He cannot lie, so we can hold on to His promises. God promised to give us the Holy Spirit to guide us into all truth (John 16:13). Hold on to that promise and come expecting to experience His presence. It's His will to have close fellowship with you (2 Corinthians 13:14).

3. Listening

Did you ever meet someone who only wanted to talk about themselves? Unfortunately, this is often our approach to God. I've found that one of the biggest keys to finding the garden is learning how to listen. We must be quicker to listen and slower to speak (James 1:19). Remember the story about my friend Ben and how he heard God's audible voice? Even though God doesn't always choose to speak that directly to us, I am convinced that He is always speaking—every day, moment by moment.

I think of it like a radio. When I'm driving down the highway in my car, the radio waves are shooting all around my vehicle. I can't see them, but science tells us that those radio waves are there. The only way I can hear that signal is if I have a transmitter that can tune in and pick it up. As soon as I flip the knob of my stereo, sound explodes out. The radio waves didn't magically appear. They were already there. I just tuned in.

Hearing God means learning His language and I've found that He usually speaks to me in a one of three ways: through the Bible, through someone else, or in a quiet inner voice. I don't want to limit God. He's speaks other ways too; those just seem to be the most common with me.

Let me explain my knowledge of this quiet voice. I've had countless young leaders pull me aside over the years and I can see the desperation in their eyes before they speak. I already have a hunch about what they're going to say. They want to know how to discern the voice of God, and how to hear His direction. Scripture is key. God never contradicts the scripture. Other mature believers are key. You've got to listen to godly council.

Then there's the third key element. I can only describe it as a "peace" or a "pulling." When I need to make a decision, and I've sought out scripture and the advice of those I trust, and still I am unsure of God's specific will, then I get alone. Above all else, I come into that time believing that God wants to speak to me and lead me. Faith releases the direction of God, so if I don't believe that He'll speak then I won't be able to hear Him.

Next, I search my own motives. I often write this down. I go through all the reasons I would want something. I try to process and understand my own insecurities and selfishness and consciously remove them from the equation. I ask for wisdom (James 1:5) and I completely surrender my will. Then I wait for God's inner pulling. I ask Him to tug my heart in the direction that He would have me go. I often find that His peace will mark the direction in my heart. Sometimes the answer isn't what I want to do. Sometimes this process takes longer than I would like. That just comes with the territory.

I am convinced that most people don't hear from God on a daily basis simply because they are unwilling to slow down and listen. If I need to make a really big decision, I sometimes set aside two or three longer times to wait on God and hear His voice. Of course, God's voice must line up with the scripture. In little things and in big things, we need to learn what the inner direction sounds like and the more you hear it, the more familiar you become with His voice.

4. Asking

The next section of my alone time is making requests of God. Asking God actually releases God's blessings in our lives (John 14:13, Mark 11:24, Matthew 7:8). Not asking means not receiving, so I try to ask big.

Here's the process I go through: I discern His will based on the scripture and the Holy Spirit and then I ask big, specific requests. For example, I know its God's desire for every human being to be saved from judgment and hell (1Timothy 2:4). I ask God to radically invade the lives of those whom I know are not saved and to lead them to salvation. I can ask because I know it's what He wants, and asking actually releases the promise.

I ask God for financial provision, protection for my family, wisdom to lead, help in my weaknesses, and tons of other things. I've learned that my Father wants me to ask. It stretches my faith and it causes me to put my requests into words and verbal speech. Scripture tells us that our words carry blessings and cursing, so verbalizing my requests releases power in the spiritual realm. Ask for things for your own growth. It's prideful not to ask, and you can't lead others where you haven't been, so we need to ask God to help us grow!

5. Interceding

When I first gave my life to Jesus, the word "intercession" was completely foreign to my vocabulary. Soon I learned that certain members of the church were called intercessors, and from my observations I concluded that interceding was only for the older women in the back of the church. I remember telling God, "Father, I'll do anything for you, and I'll go anywhere, but I don't want to sit around and just pray for people. I want to go do something."

To intercede means to plead for a cause, like a lawyer would plead before a jury on behalf of their client. In the Old Testament, the Hebrew priests were instructed by God to intercede for the sins of the rest of the nation. They stood between God and the people, just as a lawyer stands between the judge and the criminal. In the New Testament, the ancient priesthood is done away with because through Jesus, every follower of Christ is a priest. We are all given the incredible privilege to intercede.

I never consistently practiced intercession until I read the book, *Shaping History through Prayer and Fasting,* by Derek Prince and realized that my prayers could change the outcome of events. Then I read in Hebrews that Jesus had interceded and asked God for dominion over death, and it was His prayers that broke the power of death and enabled Him to walk out of the grave (Hebrews 5:7).

To intercede means to stand between God and a situation and to cry out for God to intervene. This is a huge responsibility and God has entrusted us to help bring His will to pass through our prayers. But what if we choose not to pray? Do we bare some of the responsibility for the sin and injustice around us? I am convinced that we do.

In the first two chapters of the book of Nehemiah, God gives us the ABC's of intercession. Nehemiah confessed the sins of the nation as if he had personally committed all of them, and he identified with the people as he wept and cried out to God. That's a huge key. Nehemiah sought after God until his prayers were answered. He reached a place in his heart where a non-response was not an option. God answered, and changed history through Nehemiah's prayers.

Jesus told a story about a woman who kept bothering a particular judge. She would continually come to this judge and ask for legal protection from her opponent. At first, the judge ignored her, but after a while he realized that she wasn't going away. Finally, this judge decided to grant the woman's request simply because he wants her to leave him alone! Jesus uses the story to uncover a principle. The principle is *persistence*. He's drawing a parallel between how human affairs and heavenly affairs work. In both instances, fervent persistence gets the job done. Jesus finishes the story with these words: "Will not God bring about justice for His elect who cry to Him day and night, and will He delay long over them? I tell you that He will bring about justice for them quickly..." (Luke 18:7-8a). Intercession changes the course of events.

There's a secret found only in intercession that many Jesus followers never find. As we begin to intercede for our friends, family, schools, jobs, and our nation, God allows us to experience His love for people in a deeper way. We get the chance to feel what He feels, and this enables us to act as He would act. Our hearts can become soft to the desires of God and we're pulled closer to Him.

I can often pick a true intercessor out of a crowd. They smile differently. There's a softness and brokenness in their life that makes them stand out. Because of their intercession, they have a great capacity to embody the character of Jesus.

I think that if we are honest with ourselves, most Christians don't practice intercession. We don't know what it means to cry out in faith until God moves. Just like Nehemiah and the persistent woman in Jesus' story, we need to learn the discipline of heaven-born intercession. We need to come to God in faith and cry out for His will to break into the situations of our lives.

One last thought on intercession. Sometimes of Christians, we can insulate ourselves from a broken world. We get busy with our lives and forget about the pain and garbage that our neighbors face without God. If you're in the place where you can't remember the last time you wept for the broken, then it's time to get close to the broken. Spend some time with those who don't know God and ask Him to give you a heart to pray for their deliverance. There was a time in my life when I thought that I was too busy to do stuff like that—then I realized that Jesus spent much of His time with the broken, and if the Son of God had time, I could probably fit it in my schedule.

6. Studying the Bible

I never tried to read the Bible in a year. I'm not against that—I've got friends who have the chart and plan it out and everything. My strength was never in reading fast. Early on, my approach to Bible study was this: read it, and don't go to the next verse until I understand it. As a young Christian, there were times where this was bitterly painful. I'd get stuck on some weird random verse and end up only focusing on that verse for the next forty minutes. However, it developed in me a system for breaking down scripture.

With an Amplified Bible, a Strong's Concordance, and Matthew Henry's commentary I would pick that verse apart until I at least had some clue of what God was trying to say. Everything I learned about the verse, I wrote down in a notebook that I kept with me all the time. Sometimes I'd read a chapter in an hour, and other times I would only get through a few verses.

I still read the Bible this way. I've found that deep, slow study pays off. I take time to wait and listen to what the Holy Spirit is trying to tell me, and then I always take time to write my discoveries. There's something in writing it down that makes it more concrete. My typical strategy is to focus half of my time in an Old Testament book and half of my time in a New Testament book. Some favorites are Psalms, Daniel, Joshua, Matthew, Romans and Ephesians. If you aren't already, start exploring for yourself and learning His Word.

There's a power in the Bible that is often misunderstood today. We are living in a culture that doesn't believe in absolutes and because of that even

Christians miss the power of the scripture. History, archeology, and manuscripts aren't needed to prove the Bibles authenticity. It proves itself.

Just like an owners manual for a car, when followed the truths laid out in the Bible prove themselves to be the unshakable Word of God—because they work. If we want to unlock the power of the Bible, we have to read it with the conviction that the words are absolutely true, and a commitment to align our lives with its truth. If you do this, the scripture lives and breathes and speaks.

7. Christian Literature

When I was in high school, I was never a big reader. I actually took a speed-reading course with a friend of mine just because I didn't like reading the books assigned to me in school. It didn't help much. I think that many people get turned off to reading all together from bad experiences in school. We often get assigned books that don't interest us, and then we're forced to read in front of the class and feel like a goof. As a young Christian, I wanted to pursue God with all my heart, but I still wasn't a fan of reading. I remember talking with one of my older Christian friends and they told me, "Justin, the truth is that every great leader is also a great reader." I didn't like the sound of that—but they were right.

Once I started to read things that interested me and brought me closer to God, I took off like a rocket. I devoured books left and right and today I am an avid reader. I never read to read. I read to grow. Speed doesn't matter at all. I'm a slow reader by nature, but comprehension is the key. I want to learn and change based on what I learn.

Today, I focus my reading on four separate areas. They are: relational growth, church reformation, evangelism, and leadership. These areas are specific for me because they follow my gifts and my strengths. The areas will obviously look different for you. I've put a list of suggested reading at the end of the book to get your fire started. Reading is about learning and you want to find books that are making an impact on the way you think and live.

I also try to pull key ideas from every book I read and file them, meditate on them, and keep those ideas fresh in my mind. It's important to never let your Christian literature reading take the place of your scripture reading. Both are important, but the Bible is the life source. Keep your time with the Word first.

THE DISCIPLINE

Key components to time alone with God include worship, meditating, listening, asking, interceding, studying the scripture and reading other books on spiritual growth. I know that this may seem like a lot. There are a bunch of different components here, but the strategy and theme of all of them is closeness and intimacy with God. A lot of times people have this desire to really organize their time alone with God and that's

THE GARDEN ~ 141

not wrong, but relationship by nature is fluid. It's more like a song and less like a math equation.

The most important thing to remember is that as we make our sloppy, imperfect, and often distracted attempts to connect with God, He actually does come closer. The Apostle James taught the church that if we draw near to God, then He will draw near to us (James 4:8). God loves the fact that we are pursuing Him.

There is a component of discipline that is important and I think that many Christians don't have consistent intimate time with God simply because they have not developed the discipline in their lives to stay consistent. We talk about it and commit to it, but there's a big gap when it comes to follow through. Discipline is important. There will be boring, uneventful moments where it feels like you're talking to an empty room. But if we can be disciplined to practice sports, get to work on time, and master Guitar Hero, why can't we be disciplined to draw near to God every day and be transformed?

I personally apply two little discipline tactics to help myself and those I disciple. The first is to set a specific time goal for alone time every day. If you are just starting, try fifteen minutes alone every morning with God. After you get in to a routine, move to thirty minutes, then forty-five then spend an hour alone with God. You don't want to hang out at fifteen minutes for too long.

The second tactic is to find an accountability partner. Find another Christian who is passionate about developing an alone life with God, and make a specific time commitment to them. In other words, choose an amount of time and tell them. Then make a penalty if you slack off. We've usually done cash penalties. Five, ten, or twenty bucks every time you miss a day. After the second or third time you have to pay them, even your flesh will want to spend time with God in order to avoid paying the fine!

For those reading this who are ultra spiritual, that advice may seem "unspiritual." What I've found is that when the spirit man is weak, the natural man needs a little practical incentive. Consistency and discipline are much easier to develop when you are not alone in the battle.

There's a joy found in the garden alone with God that is indescribable. It is the sweetest, most life-giving experience to meet with God and to hear the beating of His heart. The garden is God's strategy for cultivating the ideas laid out in the first half of this book. It's the time every day where these truths sink deep into your soul and change your thinking. The garden doesn't have a microwave. It's not quick and easy, but it produces lasting change. I challenge you today to go there. Find it. Seek.

Chapter 6
HOW TO GET THE WORLD'S ATTENTION

It was the year 1915 when a short unassuming Indian man returned to India with the dream of independence burning in his heart. He didn't command an army, and he hadn't made a name for himself, but Mohandas Gandhi knew that somehow he would get the world's attention. Soon Gandhi became involved in politics and started organizing peaceful protests to expose British tyranny. His efforts were obviously not welcomed, and before long, he was separated from his family and thrown in prison. This would be the first of many nights that he would eventually spend suffering for justice.

Gandhi understood that if he wanted to get the attention of the British Empire, he couldn't do it with a militant militia, but he could organize millions of Indian peasants to peacefully oppose imperial rule and reject the British way of life. He set up a boycott against all British goods, and even made his own clothing at home to protest British-made clothes. His efforts were unorthodox and radical, but soon millions of impoverished Indians joined him, and the peaceful rebellion spread like wildfire. He walked away from a life of comfort and financial prosperity as a lawyer and turned his ideas into a lifestyle. At first he was ignored, then publicly rejected, then imprisoned. Thousands who followed him were beaten and imprisoned with him, but with all the threats and prison time, the British Empire could not make this peaceful man go away. Every time they tried to silence him, Gandhi's movement grew, until his name became the embodiment of justice. Finally, stories of his non-violent protests spread beyond the boarders of India, and for a short time, his desperate plight for justice caught the imagination and attention of the entire world.

People lost track of their favorite sports teams and their companies' stock options, and the gaze of humanity was fixed on this little unassuming man who had awakened the conscience of the world. Without one gun or one bullet, India was released from British rule and Gandhi had accomplished the impossible.

How did he do it? What made his message of non-violence and Indian liberation so powerful? Was it his rousing speeches or his charismatic personality? Was it his ability to organize and plan large protests? Not hardly. There was nothing brilliant or kingly about him. Gandhi's efforts changed the world for only one reason. He was a man who had embodied his vision.

Most people hold to a set of beliefs more loosely than they'd like to let on. I'm sure you've heard people say that everyone has a price, and the truth is that most of us do. We believe things, but if enough pressure was applied, we'd likely come up with a palpable excuse to compromise our core values. But not all men and women have lived this way. Every once in a while, someone steps onto the scene who does not play by those rules. These are people who have found a cause that they're ready to die for, so they take every area of their lives—great or small—and align it with their beliefs. Because this truth is so important to them, these unique people go far beyond what would be considered normal, to the point where they no longer just believe in the cause. They become the cause.

This happens more often then most of us realize. In the early 1900's, one passionate scientist was not willing to accept the last generation's faulty theories. He pushed beyond what others had found and gave his life to understand the depths of science. He discovered some of the most groundbreaking truths in the history of our race and today, the name Albert Einstein has become synonymous with intelligence. Mother Teresa gave her life for the poor and the sick and became the embodiment of compassion. When people think of a free India, they think of Gandhi. His life has come to represent peaceful protest.

So how does this connect with our journey towards the heart of God? I began the introduction of this book by pointing out that while the church across our nation has been talking, most people aren't listening. Whether we know it or not, we have lost our voice. We can't make an impact on the world that Jesus came to save when we have spiritual laryngitis. The only way to get this world's attention again and introduce them to redemption is to rediscover our voice by embodying our vision.

What does it mean for the follower of Jesus to embody the vision? It means to live in defiance to the world's system through the daily practice of holiness.

SET APART

Holiness is one of those words that every Christian has heard. It's all over the songs we sing and the scriptures we read. The definition of holiness, however, is a little more allusive. We all sort of know what it is, and we all know that God is holy, and we know that we should be holy—but that still doesn't give us a definition.

The simple definition of holiness is to be separated for sacred purposes. To be set apart. But set apart from what? Primarily holiness means to be set apart from sin. God is holy because He is 100% separated from sin. He has zero capacity for sin, and this puts Him in a holiness category all by himself.

We are holy in our position through Christ who lives inside us. We are holy in practice as we embrace kingdom repentance. Remember the definition for repentance? It means to change your purpose; to leave behind one way of living and to fully embrace a different way of living. Holiness is the practice of leaving behind sin and all of its distortions and instead practicing truth without the twisting and distortions of sin. But there is a unique and powerful quality about holiness. When you see the real thing in the life of another person, it is absolutely captivating.

A few years before I started Holyfire Ministries, I had a small residential painting business. It was the perfect job during the summer months in between semesters of college. During this time, I was doing my best to continue my spiritual growth at work, so I started taking out books on tape from the local library. One of the first books I checked out was Billy Graham's autobiography, *Just as I Am*. The book is pretty hefty, but it was perfect to listen to while I painted ceilings and taped off trim.

As soon as I began to learn about Billy Graham's life, I was astonished by the incredible influence that God had given him. God took a farm boy from North Carolina and gave him influence with presidents and kings across the earth. Listening to the book launched me into a mini-study of Graham's life. What I found was intriguing. The power of his life wasn't in his preaching or his people skills. People who interacted with Billy Graham were profoundly impacted by something else. As soon as he walked in the room, the atmosphere changed. He had a presence about him that commanded attention. It wasn't his looks or the way he dressed. It was something in his eyes. When he looked at someone, they could sense *holiness*.

Billy Graham had radically committed his life to the daily practice of holiness and that holiness made him look different. He carried himself with a palpable sense of holiness and it got the world's attention. C.S. Lewis, the famous Christian writer once said this about holiness: "How little people know who think that holiness is dull. When one meets the real thing…it is irresistible. If even 10 percent of the world's population had it, would not the whole world be converted and happy before a year's end?" When followers of Jesus allow holiness to dig its roots so deep in their hearts that it becomes a part of them, the world around us will stand up and take notice. Holiness has a voice. It's the embodiment of the nature of God.

I want to outline in this chapter all the areas where we need to apply this separation from the crookedness of sin to our lives. Let this encourage you—it's an exciting endeavor. It may not feel that way at first, but as we practice deep, uncompromising, holiness, we regain our voice and become the light that Jesus intended us to be. And the benefits of holiness are awesome.

FROM THE INSIDE OUT

So, if we want to get the world's attention where does this process begin? It begins deep on the inside of the soul, and it begins with an unwavering commitment to humility and honesty. Humility means that you are fully aware of your inability to accomplish anything of value on your own. That may seem harsh, or a little like self-loathing, but real humility is based in the reality that human beings are irrevocably dependant on God. It's the complete rejection of self-reliance and the complete acceptance of God-reliance.

Honesty means that you aren't going to trim and shade reality to make yourself feel better. You're going to look your failures in the face and you're going to deeply search your heart for crooked motives. This inner work develops what most people know as integrity. Integrity is inner character or soundness. The more honest and humble you are on the inside, the more integrity you display on the outside.

Integrity grows through the practice of self-examination. Here's what it can look like practically. Next time you sin and do or say something contrary to what God says is true, get alone with a pen and notebook. Write down the sin as best you can. Then write down the motive behind the sin. Maybe it was selfishness, self-promotion, lust or insecurity. Try to write down specifically how you displayed this motive. Think of other ways in which this motive affects your daily decisions. Then take some time to be quiet before God. Let Him speak to you about the issue. As you are quiet before God, the motives of your heart will become clear and sin won't have anywhere to hide.

I've found that God has this way of revealing the deep things of my heart that I would never discover otherwise when I go through this process. Sometimes I act frustrated toward someone but God reveals a bigger issue of insecurity about His ability to provide. Sometimes I lack confidence but the bigger issue is a lack of trust in the fact that I'm God's son and accepted by Him. You get the idea. Things aren't always as they seem. Your heart can trick you, so you must learn to hear from the Holy Spirit to discover your real motives. I remember when I first started practicing self-examination. I had read a book by the great revivalist Charles Finney called *Lectures on Revival*. In the book, he talks about going through this process of really examining and understanding your hearts motives. It completely messed me up.

The next step after you realize the crooked motive of your heart is to confess that motive to the person you wronged and to God. It's one thing to tell someone, "I'm sorry I got angry," but it's a lot tougher to pull them aside and say, "I am sorry for my actions. I've been reflecting and I realize that I got so angry at you because I have some insecurity about my own gifts. I was acting out of selfishness and jealousy and I'm really sorry."

Can you imagine for a minute what Christianity would look life if people started making more honest heart confessions like that? What would happen if every follower of Jesus took time to deeply examine themselves on a regular basis?

Months ago, I was leading worship and preaching at a three-day conference just outside of Boston. It was the third night of the conference and I could sense that God wanted to do something crazy. There was a stirring inside my heart to see an outpouring of His Spirit. We sang a few songs and then I began to share about repentance and self-examination. Soon the atmosphere in the room started to change and a deep conviction swept over the people.

It began with just one or two people, but within a few minutes, dozens in the crowd were weeping in repentance. A sense of the holiness of God filled the room and for a long stretch of time, no one said or did anything. In the silence, all that could be heard was the deep sound of weeping. Then God whispered in my heart some instructions. I told the group that if anyone wanted to publicly confess their sin and ask for forgiveness for the wrong they had committed, they could come up to the microphone—I didn't expect the response that that I received.

All around the room people came forward and confessed the deepest secrets of their hearts and asked others for forgiveness. It went on for hours. Some shared about past failures and family hurts and others publicly asked others to forgive them. Slowly, the atmosphere in the room shifted from one of repentance to one of freedom and joy. Someone started singing a song of victory and others joined in. Before long, the entire conference was dancing around the room celebrating the freedom that humility and honesty bring!

Something happens to a person when they decide to be brutally honest about their faults. It's not that God wants us to confess our sins to everyone everywhere, but there are moments where God calls for public repentance. The key is transparency. If there are areas of our hearts that are hidden from everyone but God, those areas grow in the darkness like fungus and eventually spread the disease. On the other side, transparent people shine. They walk a little taller and they carry a purity that can be found in their eyes. They certainly stand out in a crowd.

THE REST OF THE INSIDE

Integrity begins with self-examination, but there are two other areas that need to be cleaned up on the inside. The first is our thoughts, and the second is our eyes. When I first gave my life to Jesus as a teenager, the biggest battle for me was in this unseen world of my thoughts. I had real problems focusing on anything and I usually felt condemned about some past sin. It was almost like a spider web in between my ears that wouldn't allow any clear thinking to pass through. I would let my mind wander and think through all these terrible "what if" scenarios. My thoughts were completely out of control and I knew I couldn't get far until I found freedom.

It didn't come in a day—or a week—or a month. But still it came. The process for me was all about consistency. There were two truths from scripture that especially helped me find deliverance. The first was when Paul told us to "be transformed by the renewing of your mind" (Romans 12:2). This meant that my mind could be made new, and that I had to actively choose to renew it. By memorizing and meditating on God's truth and replacing the lies that I was believing with the truth found in scripture, I could be transformed.

The second truth that broke through the hard ground of my head was where scripture says to, "Set your mind on things above, not on the things that are on the earth" (Colossians 3:2). As I began to focus my life's energy on God's kingdom, the worries and desires of this world became less and less.

I remember a few years after I had first encountered Jesus I was driving alone in my car and the thought swept over me like a tidal wave. "I don't struggle with confusion in my mind anymore...the spider web's...gone." I drove down the street weeping and rejoicing that little by little God had taken away my mind of confusion until it no longer had a hold on me!

Our minds can be pretty scary places. If they go unchecked, our thought life will lead us into absolute disaster. Every sin, every temptation and every failure, begins with a thought. The important thing for the follower of Jesus is not to be surprised when crazy sinful thoughts appear in our minds—that's the place where Satan tempts us. The important thing is to learn to attack those thoughts and replace them with truth as soon as they are recognized. As a young, passionate Jesus-follower, I used to condemn myself every time a sinful thought jumped in my head. I'd ask God to forgive me, and I'd feel like a terrible sinner. The Holy Spirit had to reveal to me that I had not sinned unless I had willfully entertained and permitted sinful thoughts.

The last area of holiness that has to be cleaned up on the inside is our eyes. Have you ever noticed how much you can read about a person from their eyes? One good look in the eye and you can often tell if someone is lying or honest, selfish or selfless, joking or serious. The eye is the gateway to the soul. It is the transition place from the inner man to the outer man.

Jesus taught His followers that the eye is actually the lamp of the body. If your eye is clear, then your whole body will be full of light (Matthew 6:22). In other words, if a person has learned to control what they look at, then they've learned to control what they think, and if they've done those two things then their life has inner integrity. Just like when Billy Graham walks into a room the atmosphere changes, when a person with pure eyes and pure thoughts walks into the room, they get people's attention because they embody the nature of God. They shine.

What does it mean to have pure eyes, and how do we develop them? The Apostle John tells us that the "lust of the eyes" is not of the Father, but of the world (1 John 2:16). To lust means to set your heart upon something and change direction because of your desire for it. I discussed in Chapter 2 how the first priority of a Jesus-follower is to be poor in spirit—this means that everything in your life is defined and submitted to the purposes of the kingdom. If you lust over something or someone, then the kingdom no longer has your heart, and lust is acting as king instead of Jesus. When we look at something and allow the desire of that thing to grab our heart, we have lusted over it. Men lust over women when they purposely look at them with sexual desire in their hearts (and women to men). People lust over cars and flat-screen TV's when we allow those possessions to

156 ~ LIVING FOR ANOTHER WORLD

take hold of our hearts and dominate our affections. To have pure eyes means to become aware of these visual lusts and then turn away from them before your eyes lock on to the temptation. One thing that Billy Graham said on this issue saved me years of confusion. He said to avoid the "second look." We often aren't looking intentionally the first look, but it's when we choose to look back for a second look that we sin.

In a world that is overly saturated in sexual images, controlling our eyes doesn't usually come easy. If you want to live this life of inner integrity, it's going to take drastic measures. The scriptures talk about making a covenant with our eyes (Job 31:1). We have to come to a place where our desire for inner holiness is so huge that we are willing to embrace the inconveniences. It may mean getting rid of your internet or signing up for internet accountability if you're bound by pornography (For more info on that go to www.xxxchurch.com and check out x3watch).

It might mean not walking around the mall or not watching certain movies that everyone else says are okay. I can't tell you how many times I've been with Christians who feel fine watching a movie that I am unable to watch. I know that there is sexual or graphic content in the movie and the Holy Spirit inside me won't permit it. I admit that there have been times where the movie seems border-line and I battle with God. I've learned and try to always practice that it is better to be inconvenienced then it to be taken down by sin. What if

I miss a really good movie? Who cares! Purity is worth missing a million borderline movies. You'll find that the less you feed the lusts of your eyes the more sensitive your spirit will become. I've heard people say, "Sex scenes and graphic violence don't bother me." This means that their spiritual senses have become calloused and numb to those things. If that's you, it's time to make a covenant with your eyes.

There is one more step that's essential to winning this battle. The Apostle James told us to confess our sins to one another, so that we would be healed (James 5:16). I'm convinced that there's a special healing and victory that comes to a person who has committed to an accountability relationship. This means that you have someone of the same gender in your life that you have been brutally honest with about your sins. You're committed to confessing to them every time you fall, and you pray for one another for victory.

I was introduced to this idea of accountability as a young Christian in the area of sexual purity and I made an accountability commitment to my pastor that I still keep today, over ten years later. That commitment has been one of the major keys to developing inner integrity in my life and keeping me free from habitual sin. If you don't have an active accountability partner, start asking God to lead you right now. Seek Him, then approach someone of the same gender, who you see often, who has a very strong walk with God and together devise your strategy for victory. I don't believe that Christians are ever too mature for this. We all need to cultivate complete transparency.

THE OUTSIDE

If we start with inner holiness and learn self-examination, purity of thought, and purity in our eyes, then we are on our way to embodying the vision. Like Gandhi, Mother Theresa, and Albert Einstein, we will no longer blend in with the crowd. But we can't stop with the inside.

A couple years ago, my band had an opportunity to play at a bar in a battle-of-the-bands. That's not our typical gig. We aren't really the battle-of-the-bands bar playing type of band but we prayed about it and decided to do it. We didn't want to win the battle-of-the-bands, we just wanted to hang out with sinners and get their attention. Finally after all the preliminary booking was done, the night came. The bar was packed and it was everything a funky bar should be. There were drunk kids passed out, guys with too much eye make-up, and the stale stench of old beer. I couldn't help but think to myself, "This is what our generation lives for?"

We loaded in our gear and waited for our sound check. It wasn't long before I realized that my friend Anthony was playing with his band in the same competition that night. They weren't a Christian band, and Anthony was doing his best to fight off his past and follow God. I knew that God had allowed our paths to cross so that we could make an impact for Jesus.

I didn't want to get on stage and shout about hell and I also didn't want to pretend that we weren't passionately in love with Jesus. Instead, I wanted to be like Jesus and hang out with sinners and change the temperature of the room. I wanted Jesus to captivate their attention. We had seen Him do it out outreaches all over the world, but I wanted to let God be God at "On the Rocks" bar that night.

What happened was unforgettable. We played our songs and I shared about Jesus and how He has transformed me. Anthony and a few of his friends were so touched that they started worshiping and lifting their hands. At the end of the last song, the place erupted with applause. We looked at each other on stage and started laughing. Drunk kids across the room excited to hear about Jesus! It was crazy. The MC got up and didn't know what to do. He just stood there, stunned and then finally said, "Wow, that was f**** deep. That was real f**** deep." He just kept saying that!

When I got off the stage, I was swarmed by desperate, hungry people. One kid asked for prayer on the spot and as we prayed, began weeping. Later, Anthony asked me to pray with him to stay close with God. It was a wild memory. The funniest thing was that the next day we found out that we had been selected to advance in the competition.

The story has a second half that I won't tell now, but that night still makes me smile. I'll never forget the puzzled look on the MC's face as we got off the stage!

Inner integrity can't stay on the inside only. That life needs to flow to the outside and manifest in our words and actions.

Controlling what we say and using our words for God's glory is a life-long pursuit. We are creatures who have a tendency to gossip, talk bad about others, and use our words to promote ourselves. As we clean up our inside, these words that offend God are easier to notice.

Submitting our speech to God is a process. Paul teaches the church to, "let no unwholesome word proceed from your mouth, but only such a word as is good for edification according to the need of the moment, so that it will give grace to those who hear" (Ephesians 4:29). Think about that for second — no unwholesome words. This means no screaming, no losing your temper. It means no bitter, overly sarcastic, cynical speech. I know some people who would never talk if you removed all those things! Instead we are supposed to give grace. What does that mean? It means that in our tone and our selection of words we extend to others unmerited favor. It doesn't mean we're push-overs, or we avoid tough conversations. It means we speak truth drenched in love.

On the other side, there are plenty of Christians who just talk to hear their own voice. They don't say things that are led by God's Spirit and wisdom. God combats that way of living by telling us to be slow to speak and quick to listen (James 1: 19). This is the kingdom way. He desires sons and daughters who know how to actively listen. God wants to build in us enough maturity to consider others more important than ourselves and let others speak before we jump in. I remember one time I was leaving a worship gathering and there was a kid standing outside smoking a cigarette. I struck up a conversation with him and asked how he was doing. Right away I felt like God had ordained the moment. The kid started talking first about his dog that died, then about his job, then about the emptiness he felt. I just stood there and listened. I didn't say a word.

Minutes passed, and soon we had been outside talking for almost an hour. Finally, this young man realized it was late and he had to go. By this time he had tears in his eyes and was telling me that he was finally at the place where he could trust God with his life. Then he looked at me and said something a little ironic. "It's been really great talking with you. You've helped me a lot." I had probably said five sentences! At this moment in time, this guy just needed an ear to listen. I could have interrupted him and got my two cents in, but I would have missed a magical moment of inner transformation in his life. There is a time to speak, and silence won't fix everything, but learning to listen and being a good listener will always attract people to you.

With the inside clean and our words submitted to God, it will only take some consistent action to embody the vision. The action we take is pretty simple, but not easy. In everything, we are to regard others as more important than ourselves (Philippians 2:3). That's God's complete action plan to get the world's attention. Notice that Paul didn't say that everyone *was* more important than you. He said to *act* that way. This is not about comparing who's more important. It's about embodying the mindset of a servant. Scripture tells us to show *unqualified* courtesy to everyone (Titus 3:2 Amplified Bible). That's crazy. It means that especially when people don't deserve it, the real Jesus follower still acts like that person is more important than them. When we do that, we model God's character, and it stops people in their tracks.

You don't lie because you don't like being lied to and you've chosen to act like the other person is more important than you. You don't cheat because you wouldn't want to be cheated and you've chosen to act like the one you would cheat is more important than you. When we become servants in everything, we uphold all of the action requirements of holiness. That night at "On the Rocks" was a combination of inner commitment to purity, speaking words about Christ, and actions that served. It allowed God to shine through in the most unlikely place. We weren't perfect in anything, but our honest desire and effort got their attention—and yours will get their attention too.

The first time I met my friends from a ministry called Youthstorm in Windham, New Hampshire, I was able to observe "Servanthood 101" in action. At that time, Youthstorm was running an internship and had about a dozen interns. These young men and women were a rare breed of radically committed Christians. They had developed a community of intense discipleship, and the values of servant hood had spread throughout the group. I can remember as these guys cleared my plate at dinner, and carried my luggage, and did anything they could to make me feel more important. I sat on the couch relaxing as these guys washed dishes, cleared other's plates and cleaned up the kitchen. It wasn't really about the actual work and it wasn't a show. They were worshipping God through washing dishes.

I've known Youthstorm for years now and I've seen that servanthood has become a way of life in their community. They embody it, and people are startled by this way of living. The cool thing is that being around people like that doesn't just make you feel special—it makes you feel selfish. Servanthood is contagious and exposing, and the more you see it, the more you want it.

THE NEW WAY

What I've been explaining in this chapter is not to be taken as a few helpful hints to live a holy life. That's not what any of us need. What I've tried to convey is an entirely new way of doing life. I'm talking about being like Gandhi and allowing the great cause to take over your life and birth a something completely new. Embodying the vision means being radically committed to holiness so that we can announce and proclaim the character of God even by walking in the room and looking someone in the eye. You carry it; you live it.

People see it in your work, in the way you talk to others, and in the way you handle money. Inner integrity and holiness carry with them a voice that gets the world's attention. This is all about leaving behind your old life and putting on a new self. It's about redefining what it means to be a Christian in the eyes of our culture. Regardless of the standards of those around you, it's about allowing integrity to seep down into your bones and make the kingdom your core. Holiness is the theme; servant hood is the method.

In the summer of 2007 I was ministering at a Christian camp in New Hampshire, and God decided to pay me a visit. It was the last night of the camp, and the week had been filled with powerful encounters with Jesus. On this final night, kids had gathered around a campfire to share the miracles God had done in their lives and commit in front of their friends to live differently. I love to hear stuff like that. Listening to young people verbalize there commitment to Christ is an awesome thing.

As I walked over to the fire, I heard the inner voice of the Holy Spirit instruct me to get alone and pray. My initial response was, "God this isn't a good time. I want to go and hear these testimonies." His inner pulling wouldn't let up, so reluctantly I turned around and headed for a quiet room.

As I prayed, God started to break my heart for young people across the world. A deep compassion came over me and I wept for the lost and the broken. I knew that I was reaching a special place and I could feel the heart of God breaking and longing for a great awakening. My prayer became personal. "Use me God. Open the eyes of a blind generation, and use me." Then, in the midst of my prayer God spoke very clearly to my heart.

"I want you to fast TV shows for a year."

The thought came out of nowhere. I wasn't thinking about TV or fasting or anything like that, but the idea had all the "weirdness" of something God would say. I'm not a huge TV watcher, so it seemed like no big deal, but still my heart resisted making a commitment like that. Strangely, my first thought turned to sports. Out loud, in that empty room I said to God, "Father, if the New York Giants go to the Super Bowl, I'm going to be bummed." Honestly, I have no idea why that was my first thought, but it was.

The Holy Spirit spoke to my heart clearly the simple phrase, "Embody the vision. Be the change you want to see in the world." I had spent that week challenging others to set themselves apart for the things of God. What if my example could challenge more people to walk away from things like TV or video games for the sake of devoting time to being with Jesus? I smiled, and told God we'd do it.

So, from August 2007 to August 2008 I didn't watch a single TV show. When the Super Bowl came around that year, and the New York Giants surprised the world and faced the Patriots, my friends started asking what I would do. What could I do? I was out there already and I couldn't stop now. I sat on the couch with my wife playing Scrabble and listening on the radio as the Giants not only went to the Super Bowl, but made sports history and defeated the undefeated New England Patriots. My friends told me it was a really good game— to watch.

Being a part of the kingdom of God means living by a different set of priorities. How can I even compare the pleasure of obeying God to watching a football game? I want to embody the vision. I want to live this thing until I shine like the sun with the light of God, and I don't want to do it alone.

There's one more step. There's an even greater place that we can go. The greater place is found when we all do it together.

A while ago, I heard someone teach on the topic of *synergy*. I wasn't familiar with the word, or the principle behind it. Synergy basically means that the combined effort of two individuals is greater than the single efforts of the same two combined. That may sound a little confusing, so let me illustrate.

I once heard a story of two strong horses. The owners found that they could pull something like 4,000 lbs each individually, but when they strapped the horses together, they didn't pull 8,000 lbs—they pulled 10,000 lbs. Something happened to the individual horse when it was strapped next to another horse and they worked together. Something changed on the inside of that horse and it pulled harder; it multiplied it's power.

These horses illustrate the magic of teamwork. When two people do something together, the results are far greater than if they did the same work separately. That means that if two people combine their efforts and experience synergy, they have the potential to accomplish far more than if they worked the same amount of time separately. Remember Henry Ford and the birth of the assembly line? Ford put all the competition to shame because people worked together and maximized their potential. It's the X factor. It's what pushes something over the top. Remember when Jesus taught His followers to minister? He never sent them out one by one. He sent them out two by two.

The same principle applies when it comes to holy living and embodying the vision of the kingdom. It's powerful when one person does it. But what happens when a small community of people begin to live by this whole new standard? What happens when people who are committed to living radically centered on Christ start doing life together? The potential moves beyond changing your life or the life of a friend and we can now begin to dream about changing the world. If one Christian really embodies the vision and lives holy, transparent, servant hood—it will turn some heads. But if hundreds and then thousands of us brush aside plastic-face Christianity and give our lives for the kingdom? Now we are talking about major social change.

It was Nobel Prize winner Margaret Meade who captured this idea when she said, "Never doubt that a small group of committed people can change the world. Indeed, it's the only thing that ever has." She was right. Alone you are a burning torch, but with others you're a blazing furnace that can't be ignored. This is God's strategy. A family and an army.

So what would happen if you and a few of your friends actually started doing this stuff? What if you whole-heartedly practiced transparency, accountability, and honesty about your motives when you're wrong? What if you began developing the attitude and actions of a servant and chose to act as if others were more important than you were? What would your family think, or people at work or at school? What kind of contagious fire could this start in your circle of friends?

I love the fact that Gandhi made his own clothes to protest British imports. That's radical. Imagine what was going through his mind as he sat down to sew his first tunic. He was a lawyer. He knew success and he'd traveled the world. I'm sure he must have questioned himself on the inside a few times and I'm sure he felt a little silly more than once.

Today, in front of us there's a generation of young people who are starving for a cause to embody. I know one girl who chained herself to the door of a bank because the bank had done something that wasn't good for the environment. Courageous—just misdirected. If someone can be so passionate about trees, how much more should we be passionate for souls? It's time for courageous Christ-followers to take hold of the great mandate given by our savior and embody the character of Jesus to show the world a cause really worth living for.

Chapter 7
TRYING SOMETHING
IMPOSSIBLE

It was a day that I will never forget. I was in my early teens and there was a guest speaker Sunday morning at church. I hadn't been a Christian very long, but I'd seen plenty of stuff that I thought was weird. People dancing, shouting, speaking in funny languages. On this particular day, the guest minister was praying for people, and many of them were falling down or crying as he prayed. I wasn't convinced that any of what I was seeing was real, but I was hungry for God. My spirit pushed me to get out of my seat and ask for prayer.

I walked up to the front of the room about as skeptical as you can get. He finished praying for someone else, stepped towards me and as he did I got this strong sensation of heat and electricity. I can remember thinking how foreign it was. Then as he touched me on the shoulder and began praying, I couldn't stand up. Before I could choose not to do it, I found myself on my back lying on the carpet.

I laid there, fully conscious and fully aware of the presence of God. Something was happening to me that my teenage mind could not fathom. I remember thinking, "This is ridiculous, I'm getting up." So I tried. The problem was I couldn't. I still can't totally explain it, but I was stuck to the floor by the power of God.

Embarrassed, I laid there and made multiple attempts to stand to my feet, but every time I did, it was as if God was sitting on my chest. I looked even more ridiculous trying to get up, so I decided to stop fighting for a few seconds. When I did, I heard the inner voice of the Holy Spirit for the first time in my life. He just simply told me to stop trying to get up. He was healing and fixing the inner brokenness of my heart.

A deep wave of peace crashed over me and I knew that God was doing something huge on the inside. As I laid there, I could sense the inner parts of my heart shifting and being restored. I stayed on the carpet for about forty minutes before I was able to get up. My doubting mind was stilled. Something had changed on the inside of me and it seemed like the insecurities and fears that had stopped me from giving God my life didn't grip me anymore. Even my hurts that had come from a broken home didn't have the same inner sting. In one day, in a little under an hour, God had just set the course of my future.

All my problems didn't vanish and all my circumstances didn't correct themselves instantly but this initial encounter with the Holy Spirit branded my heart with a passion to believe in a God who still does impossible things. My prayer time was set ablaze, and my pursuit of God made me look extreme among other young people my age. As I started reading the Bible, all the red tape was gone and a new expectancy for the fullness of God grabbed my life. I read 1 Corinthians 12 about the gifts of the Spirit and started to passionately pursue God daily to teach me to operate in the gifts.

Then came the countless nights sitting alone on my bed asking God for the gift of tongues. I would quote 1 Corinthians 14:1 where we are told to earnestly desire spiritual gifts and I'd hold on to the promise. I sat there in the silence of my room day after day waiting for the power that held me to the floor to take control of my lips. I can remember looking out my bedroom window as a teenager and watching my friends hang out and play sports. I wanted so badly to join them but something had taken hold of my affections and wouldn't let me go. I needed to find God in a bigger way.

It was months later at a youth service that one of my good friends prayed for me and I began speaking in tongues. I learned that this gift edified and strengthened my spirit (1 Corinthians 14:4). I left the meeting that night and sat alone at my Dad's condo speaking in tongues for hours. It was like a river of love was pouring out of me and the encounter pushed me to finally let go of having to understand everything. God was God and I was not, so if speaking a strange language was going to bring me closer to Him—I was for it.

The problem with the "gifts" in Christianity today is that as soon as they are mentioned, most people's minds flash to some TV evangelist who ended up being a phony. Some people don't want to give much thought to the gifts of the Spirit because their personal experience seemed forced or fake. Unfortunately, a Christian sub-culture has developed where people supposedly operate in powerful gifts, but don't practice the basics of godly character, leaving a bad taste in the mouths of those who would seek God for more.

When a preacher moves in God's gifting we often foolishly assume that he has good theology and the two don't always go together. There have been plenty of anointed preachers who ended up having thin character, but this doesn't necessarily discredit what God did through them. What we are in desperate need of is both—character and power.

I am convinced that God is changing things right now in our generation. We shouldn't have to choose between the expression of the gifts and maturity in the Word. We should have both. God is raising up people who have built a strong foundation of holiness and spiritual discipline, but can also operate in His gifts without all the fluff. I think that most of us are done with the show and want something real—and I am unwilling to settle for anything less than all of what God has made available.

Through those key encounters at a young age, God made it clear to me that He still moves in power and miracles. Now it was time for me to learn to move with Him.

I know that some people disagree on how God gives His gifts today and my response is to honor them regardless of whether we agree or not. I certainly don't claim to have all the answers and in humility and faith we can find the heart of God together. But we have to remember the emergency. Millions are running into hell, and the church is rapidly losing her voice. God forbid that we do not seek Him for every ounce of power that He has made available to accomplish the task. Let's not base our theology on tradition, or on what makes us most comfortable. Instead, let's look the New Testament in the face and believe God for all that He's promised.

After my experience with speaking in tongues, the heat turned up in my life. I became more and more hungry for God and soon other gifts started to grow. I saw people instantly healed of colds and headaches when we prayed and got impressions or "words of knowledge" from God.

One fateful evening, I decided I was ready to take a bigger step in to the supernatural.

STEP OF FAITH

At sixteen years old and full of faith, I was ready to see a big God do impossible things. My friends and I had attended a youth conference with about four hundred other young people and towards the end of the final night, we were instructed to break into smaller groups and pray for one another. I spotted a girl across the room that was in a wheel chair and decided that I was going to tell her to rise up and walk.

I went over to the girl and asked her if I could pray for her. She said I could and explained that she had injured her leg for the second or third time and would need extensive surgery. I told her that I felt like we should pray and then see if she could walk to me. We were bold and we were ready for something crazy to happen. I prayed, and she started pulling herself to her feet.

It was an intense moment. People from the conference gathered around. She took the first step, then the second, then lost balance and crumbled to the floor.

Me and one of my friends quickly helped the girl up and got her back in the wheelchair. I stood there, frozen, with my eyes glued to her face. I didn't know what to say. For a minute we just looked at each other, confused and disappointed. I apologized, but she wasn't offended. She wanted to step out and risk. Still, I was left with a theological mess and the guilt and pain of failure.

Where was the God I had encountered months before? Where was the power that had jolted my life?

As a sixteen-year-old kid on fire for God, I was pretty shaken. Why hadn't she gotten healed? Why hadn't we seen a miracle? How does this faith thing work? I knew that God was real, and that He was a God who did impossible things, but something had gone very wrong. I sat alone in the hotel conference room that night, wrestling with God and wondering how I could move forward.

People throughout my life had let me down. I had trusted them, and there were times where they hadn't come through. Now those same feelings were bombarding my mind toward the God I loved and trusted. What if God failed me again? How could I trust Him if I never knew when He was going to show up? My faith was paralyzed. I had reached a crossroads and I had to make a decision.

In that moment I decided something. It was a difficult decision that would set the course for the rest of my life. I don't understand why the sick aren't always instantly healed, but Jesus clearly instructed His followers to pray for the sick and expect them to recover.

I don't know why everyone doesn't operate in the gifts of the Spirit, but God said to earnestly desire spiritual gifts. I don't know why I was stuck to the floor for forty minutes or why I didn't speak in tongues all those nights alone in my room. In the midst of all these "I don't knows" I decided that I was going to spend my life trying impossible things and leave the results to God. I would listen for His voice, do my best to obey, and not expect to understand it all. Mystery is difficult—faith is difficult—but this is the journey we are invited on.

I've crashed and burned plenty of times, more times than I would like to admit, and I've learned a little more tact along the way, but that doesn't change the fact that this Jesus-following life is a life of risk. If I am not risking something somewhere, then I am not following the God of the Bible.

In the midst of risks and failures I have watched first hand as people have been healed, bodies have been transformed and lives have been changed. It hasn't happened every time, but it's happened--and those moments of the miraculous have left me hungry for more. There comes a point when we have to embrace the mystery and trust Him through the times we don't understand. We have to risk if we ever want to demonstrate His reality.

THE DEMONSTRATION

Have you ever met anyone who sold Kirby vacuums? Maybe you've sold them yourself. It seems that in every crowd there's always at least one or two people who've spent countless hours going door-to-door selling Kirby vacuums. My brother sold them for a while and did pretty well. They're expensive and they aren't much to look at. The first time I heard the purchase price I honestly thought that the salesman was kidding. I couldn't understand why someone would spend so much on a vacuum when Wal-Mart had fourteen other options for a fraction of the cost.

But the key to selling the Kirby is in the demonstration. It usually goes something like this: The salesman walks into the buyer's home and the buyer has no intention of actually buying the vacuum. The salesman turns the thing on and runs it across the buyers couch. He then displays the thousands of dust mites and gnats that were living in the couch that the Wal-Mart vacuum wouldn't remove. Pretty soon the buyer is feeling like they would be foolish and maybe even irresponsible if they didn't empty their savings and buy a Kirby vacuum!

Demonstration changes everything. It's takes a foolish idea and converts it in to a brilliant one. The gospel of the kingdom must carry demonstration or it's just a ludicrous, costly, dangerous, foolish idea. We as Jesus-followers are given the task of intentionally advancing this kingdom and we are told that the best way to advance it is to demonstrate.

Think about it for a second. You tell your non-Christian friend that God exists, that we are terrible sinners and that we're blinded by the lies of an evil spiritual kingdom that's invaded planet earth, and that God has purchased our redemption by coming to our planet in the form of a man and dying for our sins. Tell them that this death paid the penalty for all the sins of the world and gave all those who will believe access to spiritual salvation, physical healing, and inner deliverance. Tell them that, and see what reaction you get.

They'll probably not want to hang out with you anymore. Tell them the same thing, and then demonstrate this kingdom, and they will stand back in awe. Like the Kirby, seeing the results changes everything. How do we demonstrate it? It doesn't always mean we need to see a miracle or a healing. Demonstration also includes a life set-apart for Jesus or generosity that is beyond human kindness. In fact, a miracle without the lifestyle only muddies the water. It will almost always include stepping out in uncomfortable territory and asking God to do impossible things.

Jesus was the king of demonstration. That was key to His effectiveness. He healed the sick to demonstrate that it is God's will to heal. He broke demonic bondage to demonstrate that God is stronger than Satan. He hung out with sinners to demonstrate that people can come just as they are. He spent entire nights in prayer to demonstrate the importance of intimacy with the Father. He walked on water to demonstrate His dominion over the earth, and He died on a cross to demonstrate His undying love for humanity. Then He pointed a finger at you and me and said, "He who believes in Me, the works that I do, he will do also; and greater works than these he will do; because I go to the Father" (John 14:12).

Was He kidding? Nope. The Apostle Paul figured it out. He realized that if he could persuade someone to follow Jesus then somebody else could persuade them to stop following. So he gave up on persuasion and moved to demonstration. He said, "My message and my preaching were not in persuasive words of wisdom, but in demonstration of the Spirit and of power, so that your faith would not rest on the wisdom of men, but in the power of God" (1 Corinthians 2:4-5). This is risky, and pretty scary. It's also incredibly exciting.

When I was a junior in high school I took a class called Project Adventure instead of taking the typical gym class. Instead of playing ultimate Frisbee and softball, we would go outside and climb trees and use ropes and harnesses. The class was taught by Mr. Manchuck, a short stocky man in his mid fifties with a broad smile, iron biceps and the biggest thigh muscles you've ever seen. He wore shorts in February, and could climb straight up a tree with no branches. Everything about this class was cool and we were all relieved to get a break from another year of the same old games in gym.

The final test of the class was an intense obstacle course that wound through trees and over a river, finally leading to a long zip line. The zip line was about forty feet off the ground, high up in a skinny tree. It ran almost the length of the entire obstacle course. The student would swing onto the small platform from a nearby tree, detach their rope, and attach their harness to the zip line. Then they jump. It was a lot of fun.

Me and a few other guys in class finished early, so we just hung out by the zip line and watched everybody go. I was sitting in the grass minding my own business when another student nudged me. "Yo, have you heard about the superman?" I had no idea what he was talking about, so I asked him what it was. He went on to explain, "The superman is when you put your harness on backwards and attach the zip line to your back and jump off the platform. It's like you're flying."

That didn't exactly sound appealing to me. It sounded more like a death wish. The kid looked at me and smiled and then said loud enough so that everyone else could hear, "You should do the superman." Pretty soon, I was surrounded by a bunch of high school kids saying, "Do it, come on..."

I admit that it wasn't courage that motivated me. It was pure peer pressure. I climbed up to that little forty-foot platform in the tree and it suddenly felt like four hundred feet. My hands were sweaty. My stomach felt queasy. My leg started twitching.

I grabbed the carabineer and pulled it behind my back. Since the zip line didn't have much slack, I had to stand on my tippy-toes just to get the harness attached. Of course, I couldn't see if I had done it right. I started squirming around up there on this platform thinking that maybe I attached the carabineer to my belt loop accidentally. I was nervous—but there was no going back.

Finally, I stepped to the edge of the platform and prepared to jump. I let my feet slowly lose contact with the wooden plank and the zip line did the rest. I had to agree that "Superman" was a good name for it. I soared headfirst down that zip line with my arms out like a California condor and for a few minutes, I was Superman.

The Superman is the physical example of what being a Jesus-follower means in the spiritual. It means that you're hands will shake sometimes and your stomach will feel queasy. It means that you will do things that run contrary to logic, but it will be these exploits that shift the course of eternity.

My soul aches to see the power and anointing described in the Bible restored to the church and I am so tired of a powerless gospel that doesn't transform the human soul. I want nothing to do with it. I believe that God is restoring His power in our day, and I want to be one of those who learn to operate in that power. Not flaky, not hype--not fake. But humble, honest, transparent, and courageous.

The first sermon I can remember preaching as a teenager in a youth group was entitled, "The Big Shift." I talked about a time when Christians demonstrated the power of God to such a degree that we no longer needed to search for people to witness to. Evangelism had shifted and God's power was so evident that people sought us out and asked us, "Will you pray for me? How do I get what you have?"

Can you imagine that? Can you imagine a church where people are real, and miracles are a way of life. Where everything is done in love and Christians step out of their comfortable cages and expect God to do impossible things—that's what my heart longs for.

A few months ago I was leading worship at a Christian camp and met a young girl named Emily. I could tell she had a desire for God, but something was holding her back. As I prayed, I felt the Holy Spirit give me a word of knowledge. Understand, it wasn't this panoramic vision—although I wouldn't mind one of those. It was just a whisper from the voice I've heard a hundred times in that secret place of the garden. It's the voice every believer can hear when we seek Him.

When I had the opportunity, I shared with Emily that I felt God had given her a gift to teach and that she loved working with young children. I also told her that she had witnessed some very difficult situations with her family. I described a situation that I had seen in my mind's eye. I never had a conversation with this girl before, and these words hit her like a bucket of concrete.

Her camp counselor came to me later and said, "I don't know what you said to Emily, but she is changed. She's really focused on God since you spoke to her." This quick encounter is one tiny example, but it illustrates the point. When the gospel is shared and demonstrated, it can make the full impact God intended. One simple word of knowledge changed this girl's outlook on God and on herself.

THE HOW

We all know why the gospel should be demonstrated, but how do we do it? If God has called us to try impossible things, what way has He supplied to accomplish impossible things? I've found that the longer I am a Christian the more aware I become of my own inability. I don't have it. Nothing good dwells in me—so how do we get to the other side?

Thankfully, we can be submerged. We can be immersed. We can be overwhelmed—by the Holy Spirit. This submerging takes ordinary people and empowers them to do the impossible. Bill Bright, the founder of Campus Crusade for Christ said it well when he said, "Never forget the necessity of the Holy Spirit's power. After years of discipling, most of the disciples deserted Jesus at the cross and one betrayed Him. It was Pentecost that made the ultimate difference!"

The contrast is glaringly obvious. Before they were baptized in the Holy Spirit, Jesus' followers had seen countless miracles but still didn't have the inner strength to stand firm at the first sign of persecution. After they encountered the Holy Spirit and were submerged in His power, they became as bold as lions and operated in a powerful anointing. I don't want to sell out when the pressure is on, but the truth is that I don't trust myself to stand up. It has to be the overwhelming power of the Holy Spirit that takes a common man and makes him a courageous saint.

With the Spirit come His gifts. These gifts are outlined in 1 Corinthians 12 and other places in scripture, and we are instructed to pursue them and desire them. I think that many Christians don't operate in the gifts simply because they don't pursue them. The gifts empower us to do impossible things and access grace—power beyond our own ability. If Jesus has purchased for us the gift of the Spirit and we can accomplish the impossible through the power of the Holy Spirit, then what are we waiting for? Is there another ingredient that we're missing to launch us in to the supernatural life?

THE KEY INGREDIENT

What's the key ingredient to activating the power of the Holy Spirit? How do we take these promises from words on a page to reality that changes lives? To discover it, we need to understand the foundational principle that God has established to advance His kingdom. It's the faith principle—simple but not easy.

In American politics, men and women run for office and are elected by the people. In the case of the president, once the president is elected, he's then given the task of hiring an administration. Most people don't realize this, but the president has the responsibility of hiring over 2,000 people for his staff and cabinet before he is sworn into office. These people, along with the policies that they advance, make up the president's administration. The Bush Administration or the Clinton Administration, for example, advocated for certain policies and held to certain values. But did you know that God has an administration?

The administration of God operates on one core principle. There is one key ingredient, like oil in the engine of the automobile that allows all the other parts to work to their full potential. The Apostle Paul shared this core principle when he wrote to Timothy, "...the administration of God...is by faith" (1 Timothy 1:4). Faith—that's the oil in the engine of the kingdom of God. God uses it, and we need to use it. He created the world using faith, He went to the cross using faith, and He rose from the grave using faith. Does that mess with your thinking a little? That God uses faith.

Faith has a creative force. It gave Sarah, Abraham's wife, the ability to have a child (Hebrews 11:11). Think about that. It created the necessary physical properties for a barren elderly lady to conceive and give birth.

It creates things that didn't exist and makes things manifest in the natural that were promised in the spiritual. It's a conviction about things that are unseen. God is pleased when we have big faith. In fact I think that big faith pleases God more than anything else; and He's disappointed in us when we have little faith.

So what does it mean to have great faith in God? It simply means that the Word of God is your ultimate source of truth and reality. The unseen government and authority of God is *more real* than the visible circumstances.

In the Old Testament, Joshua walked around a city and believed that God was going to knock down the city walls when he yelled. That's wild; and it worked. Daniel believed that God was going to protect him in a den of lions and the lions never touched him. This faith thing has the potential to propel us way out of the realm of ordinary living.

When I first started my walk with Jesus, I really struggled to understand the relationship between me and God and faith. I couldn't grasp how the three of us were supposed to work together, until God unlocked the truth hidden behind a story in scripture. The truth I discovered has become one of the greatest keys in my life. The story is in 2 Kings chapter four. In the story, a widow comes to the prophet Elisha to ask for help. She can't pay her bills and the authorities were threatening to take her children as slaves in payment for her debts. The woman comes to the end of her rope and begs the prophet for help.

The first thing Elisha does is ask the woman what she has. All she has that's of any value is a single jar of oil, so from this one resource, the prophet devises a plan of faith. He tells her to gather from her friends and neighbors any jar or bucket or bin that they'll let her borrow. She sends out her sons and pretty soon her living room is full of empty jars. Elisha then instructs the woman to pour the one jar of oil into one of the empty jars. When she does this, the oil multiplies and she is able to fill every jar in her house!

Maybe you've read the story before. It has a happy ending. When the woman comes to the last jar, the oil stops. Elisha tells her to sell the oil, pay off her debts and live on the rest. It's a cool story of God's provision, and when I studied it on this particular day, there wasn't anything about the story that stood out to me. As I finished reading, the Holy Spirit broke into my thoughts and asked me a question. His voice was clear and direct. "What if she had gathered twice as many jars?"

Immediately I knew the answer, but the whole idea was strange to me. The thought was foreign to my way of thinking and my mind needed time to wrap around it. I said out loud, "She would have had twice as much oil."

The implications of that fact are life altering. *God works through the structure that I give Him.* If I give Him a big structure to work through, I'll experience a God who does big things. If I give God a small structure to work through, I will spend my entire life interacting with a small God. I'll only get a piece of who He could be in my life. If the woman in the story had gathered twice as many jars, then she could have lived on far more.

Instead, she basically paid her bills and got by. All she had to do was gather more jars!

Faith has this funny thing about it. If you develop within yourself an expectation for the impossible, then you will experience the impossible. I remember years ago, I heard a preacher challenge the crowd to pray for 100 sick people and he guaranteed that if you did, you'd see a miracle. He was right. I tried it. By the tenth person, I saw someone supernaturally healed of cancer through prayer. A few prayers later, I saw my friends tumors disappear the day before surgery. Everyone I pray for does not get healed, but some do—and I am hungry for more.

I think that one of the great diseases in our day is our little Dixie-cup sized faith. We don't expect God to do anything big, and when He doesn't we blame Him! I think that He might be saying to us, "I have done according to your faith." What if a generation rose up and believed God for impossible things? What if thousands of us together, with humility and integrity, began asking God for world-changing things and acting like God was going to do it?

BITE-SIZED GOD

Sometimes I think we read the Bible and don't connect the fact that the God we're reading about is the same God today. He's the God that took a teenager named David and made him the greatest king on the earth. He parted the Red Sea, birthed a nation out of a senior citizen, and revealed the future to a Hebrew slave named Daniel.

He's the God who used a cowardly fisherman to heal the sick with his shadow and a murderous Pharisee to preach to the Emperor of Rome. He makes slaves into kings and is in the business of surprising humanity with His power. In an age where science is worshiped and education has the final say, the world needs Jesus-followers who act like their God is transcendent and all-powerful. If God works through the structure that I give Him, then I'm going to give Him the biggest structure imaginable. Why not believe that He will use you to change the world? Why not act like God is who He said He is? What do we have to lose?

I've thought a lot about that night at the conference when I picked up the girl from the wheelchair. I asked myself a thousand times why she wasn't healed, and I don't know for certain the answer. I'm okay with not knowing.

One thing I do know is that my faith was young and had little substance. I was trying to stretch it to believe God for the girl to walk, when personally I was still struggling inwardly to believe God to forgive my sins. If I've learned anything I've learned first that we can grow our faith. Second, it grows incrementally—step by step.

We grow our faith by hearing the word of Christ (Romans 10:17). The more your ears hear the truth, the more your heart takes hold of it. Something powerful happens when we speak. Scripture tells us that God actually spoke the world into being. He was speaking things that did not exist into existence. The trick is that faith isn't like steroids. You're not weak in faith one day and then have super-sized faith the next day. Like developing muscles in your body, it grows step by step.

The other problem is you leak. You leak faith, so if you don't consistently fill yourself with the truth of God and take hold of it in your heart, it will leak out. I've found that the best way to build my faith is to first take inventory. I'll try to figure out where I am and look at my own heart to discern my faith level. Then I believe for something just beyond my faith level. Not ten times beyond my faith level—if I try that I won't have the real substance and conviction to see it come to pass. Then I try to find the promise of God that I can hold on to, and I ask God for it in prayer.

Jesus told us to believe that we have received what we've asked for, and it will be granted to us (Mark 11:24). That statement is incredible. He also said that all things are possible to the one who believes (Mark 9:23). What do you think "all things" means? I think it means *all things*.

A WILD FIRE

People throughout history have always loved to run. From the beginning of humanity, people have competed in every sort of race that we could conceive in our minds. We love competition. From the time of

Adam and Eve until the early 1950's, no human being had ever run a mile in under four minutes. Many had tried hundreds of thousands of times. Doctors said it was impossible. Sports fans said that it would never happen. The human body just couldn't do it. People were fast, but not that fast.

Then on May 6, 1954 Roger Bannister ran a mile in 3 minutes and 59 seconds. He accomplished something that was physically impossible in the minds of millions. At age 25, the Oxford medical student made history.

But, the story doesn't end there. Within one month of Bannister's impossible world-shaking accomplishment, another runner had beaten his record. Within a few years, numerous runners had broken the four-minute mark and today, college students run a mile in under four minutes in practices. How is that possible? It seems that something Roger Bannister did made other men faster.

Faith is contagious. When one person begins to approach God with a bigger jar and expects Him to fill it, others around him will go get bigger jars too. Roger Bannister just made other men believe that they could do it. They had tried before, but they hadn't believed. Now they thought, "If Bannister can do it, why not me?"

If God can use David, Paul, Elisha, Peter or Moses, why can't He use you and me? They were just people with a nature like ours. What would happen if we began to introduce a new standard of what it means to be a

Christian? A standard that expected the fullness of God in every area of life at all times. A standard that was not content or satisfied with half-way. If you introduced this standard to people in your circle of friends, it could take route in their thinking, and they could spread it to others.

I haven't stopped trying impossible things. I'm going to keep this up until I die. I shared with you about the girl in the wheel chair and how she fell, but years later I saw her again and she walked up to me and gave me a hug. She didn't need the wheelchair anymore. A few surgeries and a lot of prayer had allowed her to walk again. Why wasn't she healed in that hotel conference room? I don't know. But I am sure that God heard the honest prayer of an immature kid who tried something impossible.

A couple months ago I was speaking at a conference for young people. During a time of worship, I felt the Holy Spirit speak to my heart. I had the faith to take a risk so I told the crowd what I was hearing. "I think that there's someone here tonight who has injured their left elbow playing baseball. If that's you, I want to pray for you tonight because God is going to heal you."

I was bold, and I was a little nervous. I hadn't had a vision or anything. It was just a faint inner impression. After the music, a young man approached me and asked for prayer. He told me that he had hurt his left elbow playing baseball and that the doctor said he tore some specific tendon. He couldn't play for the entire season. I prayed for him, and then asked him how it felt. He said that it still felt pretty much the same. That wasn't what I was hoping to hear, but I told him to keep trusting God, and continued with the night.

A few months later, I was speaking at a different church in a different state. The same young man walked up to me and reminded me who he was. I had forgotten about it, but he reminded me how I had called him out and prayed for him, and the impression from God came back to my mind. He went on to tell me how the next morning he woke up and all the pain was gone. He went to the doctor and they did x-rays of his arm. The rip in his tendon was gone and his elbow was stronger than before the injury! The doctor had no explanation. With tears in his eyes, he said, "I've been able to play baseball this season, and I hit a three-run homerun last game. I can't believe that God would do this for me."

I talked with his youth leader afterwards and he said that he's never seen this young man so on fire for God before. God used this situation to reveal Himself and set a willing heart ablaze!

In the first chapter of this book I told you about the day my ministries motor home caught on fire on route 73 East in New York and we lost over fifty thousand dollars in equipment and personal belongings. I didn't tell you the end of the story and I thought that this would be an appropriate place to fill in the blanks. We went back to Lake Placid that night after the fire and I got alone to pray. I wept and cried to God. I was glad to be alive, but I didn't know what to do about all the stuff we lost. We had an outreach concert in Fitchburg Massachusetts in four days and I had a team of eight people without clothes, phones, guitars, computers, or even a bus to get us there.

In that moment, God whispered to my heart. "This is your promotion." I thought to myself, "Not funny God." After some more time in prayer, I felt like God wanted us to write down everything we had lost and the amount of money it would take to replace each item. We got out the paper and all made huge lists. Our personal belongings alone totaled $36,000. Then we prayed to a God who does impossible things and asked for a miracle.

We got to Fitchburg four days later with borrowed instruments in a borrowed vehicle and we didn't miss a single event that summer. Within 42 days of the fire, so many donations had come in from friends and supporters across the country that we were able to replace every item that was lost with new and better stuff. Within five months, we had purchased a new vehicle and God had used this tragedy to prove Himself mighty.

One year later, we visited the site where our RV burnt down. The road was still blackened and charred so the spot was easy to find. This time we gathered, not in fear, but instead in awe. We serve a God that specializes in impossible things, so why not take the jump and believe Him for all that He has promised?

Chapter 8
PURSUING THE FULLNESS

It was the year 1891 and Evan Roberts was a teenager living in Laugher, Wales. He was unknown to the world and would stay that way for the next thirteen years. When all of his friends went out to go sailing or play sports, Evan usually wouldn't go. It wasn't that he was sick, or that he didn't enjoy doing those things. For some reason, by God's sovereign grace, Evan Roberts had been taken captive by a spiritual hunger that his generation had never seen. He wanted God's fullness— and nothing else would satisfy.

Thirteen years went by and this young man never missed a prayer meeting. By 1904, at the age of twenty-five, most people thought that Evan Roberts was at best a little strange. And he was. It was around this time that he started having encounters with God in the night, and would often stay up praying until the sunrise. On September 29, 1904, things came to a head at a prayer meeting. Evan began to cry out to God, "Bend me, bend me," as he fully surrendered his heart and his will. God heard his prayer, and the stage was set for revival.

A few days after Evan's encounter, he met with his best friend Sydney. The conversation seemed typical until Evan broke in and asked his friend, "Do you believe that God can give us 100,000 souls now?" The question was bold and Sydney later said that Evan's face was shining with a powerful light. His conviction and passion were irresistibly contagious. Sydney had to believe him. He did believe him—and the rest is history.

Within nine months of that conversation, Evan and Sydney saw over 100,000 people come to Christ and watched what historians called the Welsh Revival circle the globe. Thousands of people traveled to Wales to experience this outpouring of God, and Christians across the nations were set ablaze through the revival. These young radicals had caught a glimpse of the fullness and it went off like an atomic bomb around the world.

What is God's best for you and me? How much does He really make available to us? I'm convinced that there is a fullness that the follower of Jesus can obtain and there is a way to get there. The Apostle John tells us in his gospel account that, "of His fullness we have all received, and grace upon grace" (John 1:16). He says that God has given us the five offices of ministry "for the equipping of the saints for the work of service...until we attain to the unity of the faith, and of the knowledge of the Son of God, to a mature man, to the measure of the stature *which belongs to the fullness of Christ*" (Ephesians 4:11-13 emphasis added). Why would Paul say we could attain it if we couldn't attain it? Why would John say we've received it if we hadn't received it?

For some, Christianity is simply a way of being forgiven for the sin we commit again and again. Others take it a step further and realize that Christ is able to free us from the power of habitual sin. Only rarely, when men like Evan Roberts come along, do we see someone who asks God for it all.

As I've studied this idea of God's fullness, my journey found its footing in Romans 8:30. Paul writes, "And these whom He predestined, He also called; and these whom He called, He also justified; and these whom He justified, He also glorified." On one particular day, I found myself stuck on the end of the verse, unable to come to terms with what it was saying. *Glorified*? I thought I was supposed to glorify God, not have Him glorify me.

The whole idea didn't make any sense, so I thought that maybe the glory part of the verse would apply only after I died and passed into eternity. But Paul didn't say, "He will glorify," he said, "He has glorified." So what does it mean to be glorified?

It means that the greatest purpose of God for humanity is to bring us to a place where we carry the full honor and power of Jesus. It means that the Holy Spirit who lived in Jesus and lifted Him out of the grave lives in me. I don't have a mini-Holy Spirit and Jesus had the full-sized Holy Spirit. Since His Spirit lives in me, the honor, power, and life of Jesus can shine through me in the same way that it came through Jesus Himself. This is why He said that we would do the works He has done, and greater works. God's entire plan for the human race wasn't to forgive us and set us free from sin—that wasn't the actual heart of the plan. That was the means to accomplish the plan. The plan was to put His glory on the inside of us and permit us to carry His fullness.

It gets even clearer. Paul tells us plainly, "It was for this He called you through our gospel, that you may gain the glory of our Lord Jesus Christ" (2 Thessalonians 2:14). Gaining the glory of Jesus is the entire reason that He's called us. He didn't call us so that we could sit in a pew, or serve in Sunday school, or play on the worship team. There's a much bigger, broader, more brilliant plan. A plan to glorify us.

Understand that we gain the glory, but we don't gain our glory. We gain the glory of Jesus. In others words, we are allowed to operate in a glory that we don't deserve. When demons encounter a Christ-follower who understands the fullness and takes hold of it by faith, they must honor that individual the same way they would honor Jesus Himself.

It's not our glory—we carry His glory. When God the Father hears the prayer of a Christ-follower who is accessing the fullness, it is as if Jesus Himself prayed the prayer. This is why Jesus taught His disciples to pray in His name. This is why Paul called himself an ambassador, or representative of Jesus. We are given the highest honor that could ever be given to any created being. His power has given us everything pertaining to life and godliness (2 Peter 1:3).

The reality of the fullness changes the potential of the Christian life. We can't earn it. There's nothing we can do to deserve it. But, in order to taste the fullness in this life, we must aggressively pursue it.

THE PURSUIT

On October 13, 1972 a plane crashed in the Andes Mountains. Forty-five people were on the plane and within a few hours after the crash there were only twenty-eight still breathing. The survivors found themselves in a living nightmare. With little food, inadequate shelter, and no means of communication, they struggled to stay alive among the snow and debris. As more people died every day and the possibility of a rescue started to fade, the survivors became desperate. The altitude where they had crashed in the mountains was so high that it produced in them an insatiable hunger. After days without food, these broken, desperate people were driven to eat the flesh of those who had died in the crash in order to avoid starvation.

This story is the worst case of physical desperation that I can conceive. I can't imagine the battle that these survivors faced as they lay huddled together at night starving and freezing. They came to a place where their hunger had to be satisfied, and their lives had to be sustained at any cost.

The physical desperation that they experienced mirrors the spiritual desperation of Evan Roberts. He came to a place where the fullness of God had to be released. The power of God had to be revealed. To be alive and not experience God's fullness on the earth was not an option. It had to come—and it did come.

There is something that changes when people become desperately hungry for God. The barriers are pushed back and the windows of Heaven are opened wide. Something shifts in the supernatural when God finds an individual who will not accept anything less than His fullness.

Maybe you've experienced the sting of spiritual desperation. I know I have. As a young teenager learning about God, I started experiencing a hunger that was completely foreign to me. As soon as I realized that I could find God if I would find time to seek Him, my life became a pursuit for Him. I would set my alarm clock for 5:45 am, and open my windows in the winter to allow the cold air to wake me up. Then I would get on my face and pray.

Half the time I was distracted and plenty of other times I fell back asleep. My knowledge of God was confused and my knowledge of the scripture was minimal, but God heard the desperation of my heart. This is what it takes. There is more to be had. There is more to be found—there is more. We can know God to the extent that we pursue Him and the only barrier is our own desire.

THE PROMISE

Have you ever encountered a promise in scripture that set your heart ablaze? My fire was lit by Jeremiah 29:13 where the prophet writes on behalf of God. God tells us, "You will seek Me, and find Me when you search for me with all your heart."

This is a guarantee that the God of the universe can be found and known if only someone would give his entire heart to the pursuit. The word "search" in this verse literally means to tread and it's a word that paints a picture. The word could be used to describe a field that someone walked across day after day. After a while, the traveler would wear a path through the grass. To search for God with all your heart means to wear a path to God. It means to come to Him often and to come to Him consistently. If we do this, there is no limit to what we can obtain.

The promise gets better. Isaiah tells us that God will pour water out onto the thirsty and floods on the dry ground (Isaiah 44:3). Jesus tells us that if we hunger and thirst for righteousness, we will be satisfied (Matthew 5:6). If we do not see the fullness of God in our lives it is not because God refuses to give it. Instead, it's because *we have been content to live without it.*

I love hearing stories of those who pursue God radically. Years ago, I read about William Seymour, a one-eyed black man whose parents were slaves. Seymour had everything in life against him, but his hunger for God was uncontainable. He read in the scripture of the outpouring of the Holy Spirit and decided that he would seek God until he experienced all that scripture promised.

Seymour devoted five hours a day to prayer and seeking God, and he kept this up for 2 ½ years. At the end of the 2 ½ years, he asked God why he hadn't obtained what his heart desired. He felt God tell him to pray more! So, for another 1 ½, William Seymour prayed seven hours a day. Then, the power of God fell, the Azusa Street revival was born, and God used William Seymour to change the world.

I shared with you in chapter 3 about my friend Ben the football player, and how he heard the voice of God concerning his identity. Years later, we both finished college and Ben moved home to North Carolina. He called me on the phone one day, and shared with me something he felt God was saying to him.

For weeks, during times of prayer, Ben would sense in his spirit the number "412." He had been asking God what it meant and he wasn't sure. Was it a scripture reference, or a geographical location? What could these numbers mean?

Finally, he felt like God had whispered the answer. God was asking Ben to wake up and pray at 4:12 in the morning. I don't know about you, but I'd have to hear God pretty clearly to get up at 4:12 in the morning! Ben asked me what I thought and I told him, "Why not give it a try?"

What I love about Ben is that he went for it. So often, we will attend a good meeting or hear a good speaker and make commitments to do radical things to pursue God. Usually, those commitments fade in a week or a month. God is not condemning us for past burn-outs, but He is looking for those who will learn the discipline of passionate pursuit when no one else is watching. If it's true that we will experience God to the degree that we hunger for Him, then let's dare to pursue God with everything.

RUNNING WITH OTHERS

My passionate pursuit of God took off when I was invited to a prayer meeting at a friend's house. I was a new Christian and I didn't know what to expect, but I wanted more of God, so I decided to give it a try. At first, the entire experience was a little awkward. There were probably five or six of us, and no one was over seventeen. We didn't know how to run a prayer meeting, so we all sat down in an upstairs living room and started singing and praying. I think everyone felt funny, since we had only known "organized" prayer meetings, but the funniness soon dissolved under the roar of hunger generated by our honest prayers.

For the first time in my life I stopped caring about what I looked like or sounded like. I just allowed my heart to sing to God and cry out for more of Him. I think everyone else was feeling the same way, and within a few minutes, God's presence was so strong and so real that we all just sat there in awe. Minutes went by, then hours went by, and we lost track of time. The prayer meeting eventually ended and we decided to all get together again. For months on end, this little group met at least once a week with no agenda or plan. I started bringing my guitar, and we would all sing from our hearts towards God. I didn't know many Christian songs so we would often just make stuff up. It was sloppy, but it was real and I learned through these little meetings that pursuing God with others makes the fire multiply.

Time went by and I went to college and spent a couple of years living at school. We started a little fiery prayer meeting that met outside in the middle of campus every weekday at 7:30 am. It was a college student's worst nightmare—but we were hungry. My senior year, after some prayer, I decided to move off campus and get an apartment with three other Christian guys. This would turn out to be "Living in Community 101" for the four of us.

We wanted to live our faith to the extreme and spark a passion in other guys, so soon after the four of us moved in, we decided to let another friend live on our couch. Then one of my roommates led a kid to Christ at work, and he needed a place to stay, so he came to live on our living room floor. Then a friend's cousin from Arizona moved to our town and really needed to be around other Christians, so he came to live with us too. Then there was the kid who was dealing drugs and living with his pregnant girlfriend who got saved at our church. He needed somewhere to go, so he moved in with us. My friend Richy moved in to get his walk with God back on track, and Anton moved in because he felt like God was leading him to be around us. Before we knew what hit us, the four guys who were paying rent were in way over our heads.

It was awesome. Character was forged, accountability was established, and chaos was the anthem of the apartment. My fiancée, who later became my wife, wouldn't even go in the bathroom, but in the midst of the chaos, God was teaching us to love one another and to pursue Him together. All of our lives were changed through this year of trials and growth and I think that we all pressed closer to God together than we ever would have separately.

I developed a love for real community and today our entire ministry lives, travels and works together. Pursuing God with others is one of the most powerful dynamics that Jesus offers His followers. Scripture tells us that two people can sharpen each other, just like one piece of iron can be used to sharpen another piece. It's difficult to slow down your pursuit of God when you're constantly surrounded by others who are hungry for Him.

In many ways, you are who you're with. Bad company can cool down the most fiery Christian and good company can raise the lukewarm from the dead. If we are serious about living with new eyes on a new road, then we need to be serious about doing it together.

Earlier in this book, I described John the Baptist as one of the great examples of a kingdom-focused person. He was poor in spirit, he was fixed on eternity, and he was a deep lover of God. I mentioned how one scholar described the followers of John as, "A surging crowd of restless eager spirits, sons of a new time, impatient of worn out creeds." What if you and I took the principles discussed in this book as seriously as John took them in his day, and started to develop communities of Jesus-followers who were dedicated to the idea of living for another world? Could these communities revive the church and reach the lost, and be used by God to usher in a great awakening? It's not flashy and it can't be put on a business card, but these grass-roots communities would have the potential to change the world.

THE NEW WAY

I don't know about you, but something is aching in my soul. I can't go back to Sunday morning, production-driven, turn-it-off-on-Monday, Christianity. I can't look the emergency in the face and walk away unchanged. I can't see my backwards priorities and not be moved by the nearness of eternity and I can't know that I have the opportunity to find the garden with God, but never take advantage of that opportunity.

Someone has to stand up and live differently. Someone has to find the real substance of Christianity and restore the voice of the church. I want to be a part of that and I want you to come with me. I want to really live for Jesus and I want to chase after God's fullness. I want to see holiness restored to the church and I want to see real community where people live for others and give to those in need. I'm convinced that together we are getting closer and that God can change things rapidly. Our moment is approaching and it's time to develop this lifestyle while no one is watching, so that God can raise up fresh voices to show the way.

I want to invite you into a new way of living. It's a life that dreams big dreams, and takes big risks; a life that sacrifices to find the fullness and simplifies to stay in the garden. It comes with new priorities and with a voice that the world can hear. Like Christopher Columbus and his discovery of a new world, or like Gandhi and his embodiment of the vision, there is a new horizon for us to reach in our generation.

Two thousand years ago, the Son of God stood in front of a Roman official and told him that His kingdom was not of this world. Jesus shattered our compartmentalized view of life and challenged us to put everything in one basket. He taught us to make life simply and completely about Him. Every moment of the day, every passion of my heart—set upon Him.

Today in our generation, God is giving us the opportunity to throw away the fake version of Christianity and replace it with a holistic, all-consuming, kingdom view of reality. He's asking us to change our purpose—at all times in every area of life and leave behind the rhetoric and the routines to find the substance of real Christianity. Our generation depends on it.

I often think of the cloud of witnesses that the writer of Hebrews mentions. I think of Moses, Abraham, Paul and Peter all with front row seats in eternity. George Whitefield is there, and Evan Roberts, and all the great revivalists of the past. They're watching to see how this final scene will play out; to see what we will do with our chance. Some of our loved ones are up there watching. You and I are here, on the other side of the veil, with a brief opportunity to change history and impact eternity. We have only a moment—but this is our moment.

NOTES

CHAPTER 1
THE EMERGENCY

Ron Luce. *Battle Cry for a Generation.* David C. Cook. Colorado Springs, CO. 2005. Pg. 30
Michael L Brown. *Revolution The Call to Holy War.* Regal Books. Ventura, CA. 2000. pg 10.
http://www.encyclopedia-titanica.org/
http://en.wikipedia.org/wiki/RMS_Titanic
George Barna. *Revolution.* Tyndale House Publishers. February 2006. Pg 32.
Heroic Faith. John Harper Story. W Publishing Group. Nashville Tennessee. 2002. Pgs. 140-143.

CHAPTER 2
CHANGING PRIORITIES

http://www.elizabethan-era.org.uk/christopher-columbus.htm
http://www.eyewitnesstohistory.com/columbus.htm
http://en.wikipedia.org/wiki/Paradigm_shift
Haweis, H R, M. A. "The Age in Which the Baptist Ministered." The Biblical Illustrator. PC Study Bible v4
Thomas, John. 1985. "That Hideous Doctrine." Moody Magazine.

CHAPTER 3
FINDING THE REAL YOU

Marshall, Frank. Spielberg, Steven. 1991. *Hook*. United States: TriStar Pictures.
http://www.apl.org/history/houdini/biography.html

CHAPTER 4
BECOMING INTENTIONAL

Stephen Mansfield. *Forgotten Founding Father*. Highland Books. Nashville, TN. 2001.
Pollock, John. George Whitefield and the Great Awakening. Lion Publishing Corp. Belleville, Michigan. 1972.

CHAPTER 5
THE GARDEN

Miles, Austin. "In the Garden." Methodist Hymn. 1912.
Wurmbrand, Richard. *Tortured for Christ*. Living Sacrifice Book Company. Bartlesville, OK. 1998.
Prince, Derek. *Shaping History through Prayer and Fasting*. Whitaker House. New Kensington, PA. 2002.

CHAPTER 6
HOW TO GET THE WORLDS ATTENTION

Attenborough, Richard. Attenborough, Richard. 1982. *Gandhi*. United States: Columbia Pictures.
http://www.sscnet.ucla.edu/southasia/History/Gandhi/gandhi.html
http://en.wikipedia.org/wiki/Mohandas_Karamchand_Gandhi
Graham, Billy. *Just As I Am*. Harper Collins. New York, NY. 2007.
Finney, Charles G. *Lectures on Revival*. Bethany House Publishers. Minneapolis MN. 1988.
xxxchurch.com X3 Watch.

CHAPTER 7
TRYING SOMETHING IMPOSSIBLE

Richardson, Michael. *Amazing Faith*. Waterbrook Press. Colorado Springs, CO. 2001. Pg. 139.
Bonnke, Reihhard. *Evangelism by Fire*. Kingsway Publications, United Kingdom. 1996.
http://www.achievement.org/autodoc/page/ban0bio-1
http://www.britannica.com/EBchecked/topic/52094/Sir-Roger-Bannister

CHAPTER 8
PURSUING THE FULLNESS

Joyner, Rick. *The World Aflame*. Morning Star Publications. Pineville, NC. 1993.

Piers, Paul Read. *Alive*. Avon Books. New York, NY. 1974.

Kennedy, Kathleen. Marshall, Frank. 1993. *Alive*. United States. Paramount Pictures.

Lake, John G. *John G. Lake*. Kenneth Copeland Publications. Fort Worth, TX. 1994. Pg 88.

Haweis, H R, M. A. "The Age in Which the Baptist Ministered." The Biblical Illustrator. PC Study Bible v4

S UGGESTED READING

Shaping History through Prayer and Fasting, Derek Prince
Revolution, George Barna
Revolution: A Call to Holy War, Michael Brown
Battle Cry for a Generation, Ron Luce
John G. Lake: His Life, his Preaching, his Boldness of Faith,
John G. Lake/Gloria Copeland
No Compromise: The Life Story of Keith Green, Melody
Green
Mountain Moving Faith, Kenneth Hagin
Why Revival Tarries, Leonard Ravenhill
America is too Young to Die, Leonard Ravenhill
God's Generals, Roberts Liardon
Good Morning Holy Spirit, Benny Hinn
The World Aflame, Rick Joyner
The Normal Christian Life, Watchman Nee

FOR MORE INFORMATION ON RESOURCES OR HOSTING HOLYFIRE MINISTRIES:

Holyfire Ministries
P.O. Box 3182
New Haven CT 06515

203.887.3141
admin@holyfireministries.com

www.holyfireministries.com
www.outofhidingmusic.com
www.agenerationtransformed.blogspot.com